I0813750

STILL
ME

Praise for
STILL ME

"John Alan Turner has the mind of a scholar and the heart of a pastor. I love this guy!"

—Eric Metaxas, best-selling author of *Bonhoeffer* and *If You Can Keep It*

"*Still Me* does what so many books wish they could do: be smart, funny, challenging, and, most importantly, honest. It offers more than flippant, Sunday school answers about what God is up to in your life. Find a friend, teacher, and beautiful storyteller in John Alan Turner as he journeys with you and shows you how God is shaping and transforming you today, right where you are."

—Sean Palmer, teaching pastor at Ecclesia Houston, author of *Unarmed Empire: In Search of Beloved Community*, and featured writer at Missio Alliance

"John Alan Turner has the soul of the most compassionate pastor and the drive of a CEO. He will inspire you to be your best self and motivate you to accomplish whatever you've been putting off. His humor will keep you reading. His optimism will make you smile. And his wisdom will open your eyes to a whole new way of thinking."

—Sally Gary, Founder and Director of CenterPeace and author of *Loves God, Likes Girls*

"John Alan Turner has always been a good writer, but with *Still Me*, he is working harder than ever. I'm inspired by his honesty, and I can only hope this is the future for authentic Christian leadership."

—Hal Runkel, *New York Times* best-selling author of *Screamfree Parenting* and *Choose Your Own Adulthood*

"Some authors give us theology, others values, and others concrete suggestions for life. What we need is someone who brings all three together. John Alan Turner does just that."

—Scot McKnight, Professor of New Testament, Northern Seminary, and author of *The Jesus Creed*, *A Fellowship of Differents*, and *The Blue Parakeet*

"John Alan Turner's raw and breezy style brings biblical characters to life—on your own block, in your own skin. At the same time, he also deftly unveils some transformative glimpses of God, glimpses that may hold your gaze for a lifetime."

—Lynn Anderson, President of Hope Network and author of *They Smell Like Sheep*

Life as a Work in Progress

JOHN ALAN
TURNER

STILL ME
Life as a Work in Progress

ISBN 978-0-89112-575-4

Printed in the United States of America

Published in association with Jones Literary, Nashville, TN.

Cataloging-in-Publication Data is on file at the Library of Congress, Washington, DC.

Cover design by ThinkPen Design
Interior text design by Sandy Armstrong, Strong Design

Leafwood Publishers is an imprint of Abilene Christian University Press
ACU Box 29138
Abilene, Texas 79699

1-877-816-4455
www.leafwoodpublishers.com

18 19 20 21 22 23 / 7 6 5 4 3 2 1

To Tiffany . . . of course.

CONTENTS

ACKNOWLEDGMENTS

This is the most personal and honest book I have written, and as much as I would like for you to think I did this all by myself, the truth is much more complicated than that. I had help—lots of help. And I would be remiss if I did not take a moment now to thank the folks who got me where I am now.

That means you, Jeremy and Les and Pat and Sally and Chad and Bruce and Dan and Lisa and Phil and Jerry and Janna and Adam and Jeff and Anissa and Gabriel and Jon and Tracey and Walter and . . . well, you get the picture.

There are also people I should mention because I've stolen things from them—more things than I can remember. I'm talking about Richard Rohr, John Ortberg, Scot McKnight, Conrad Gempf, and Philip Yancey. More than words or phrases, I've stolen from them a way of thinking. I won't be giving it back, but I wanted to confess here.

There are some great thinkers, now departed, to whom I am deeply indebted: C. S. Lewis, Dallas Willard, and Lewis Smedes. I never met any of them, but I am looking forward to it in the life to come.

I owe an incredible debt of gratitude to Sean Palmer. He's more than my cohost for the *Not So Black and White* podcast; he's a trusted friend and confidant.

I have the best agent I could ask for: Jason Jones. He concentrates on the business side so that I can just write and not have to worry—that is an amazing gift. Also, he has good taste in beverages.

Thanks to Jason Fikes, Rebecka Scott, and the entire team at Leafwood for their faith and patience. I have never been treated so well by a publisher, and I look forward to seeing how God uses this partnership to bless people.

Special thanks to David Blackwell, Dane Booth, and Hal Runkel for knowing where all the skeletons are and refusing to tell anyone about them.

My daughters, Anabel, Eliza, and Mia, are old enough now to know that their dad isn't as together as he once led them to believe. I am so grateful to them for accepting me, flaws and all.

To my therapist Bill Harkins, who saved my life more than once and encouraged me to write this stuff down.

And finally, to Tiffany, who loved me better than anyone else ever has.

CHAPTER ONE

WHO AM I?

My name is John Alan Turner, and I am many things:

A writer. A published author. A theologian.
A leadership consultant. A sought after public speaker.
A teacher. A father. A son. A brother. A neighbor. A coach.
A friend. A boss. A colleague. An employee.
I am somebody's boyfriend. I am somebody's ex-husband.
I'm a survivor.
Some people love me. Some people hate me. Some people miss me. Some people wish I would go away. I wish I could say that doesn't bother me and be the person who is so well differentiated that I do not care what others think of me. That is not the case. I care. Sometimes, I probably care too much.
I am a thinker. An introvert. A storyteller. A wordsmith.
A raconteur. A whiskey drinker. I am a charmer. A flirt.
A liar and a thief. An adulterer and an idolator.
I am overly competitive. I am insecure. I am impure.

I am lazy. I'm a quitter. A cheater. A worrier.
A foul-mouthed gossip. A sinner.
I'm a man in my late forties. A child of the '70s who came of age in the '80s and married in the '90s.
I am white. I am male. I am American. I am a Southerner.
I'm conservative. I'm Christian.
More specifically, I'm evangelical—if that means anything anymore. I am not very patriotic. I may be Anabaptist. The line between those two keeps getting more and more blurry to most people, even as it becomes clearer to me.
I'm a foodie. A sports fanatic. A jazz enthusiast.
I'm an INTJ. A gregarious introvert.
A high I on a DISC profile.
I'm an Ideator. Or, if you prefer Enneagram speak, I am a 5 with a 6 wing.
I am smart. I am funny. I am generous. I'm a good listener.
I've been told I'm a good kisser. I am afraid. I am lonely.
I am disappointed and disillusioned. I am tired and frustrated.
And I am tired of being me.

I am none of these things; no one is ever always anything. I am all of these things. And I am more. I am more than my résumé, my genetics, my educational background, my preferences, my accomplishments, my failures. At least, I'm supposed to be. And I have no idea how I got here.

That's not entirely true. I could, if given enough time, probably trace a reasonable facsimile of the events that transpired, bringing me to this station in life. But who has time for that?

As I read that back I realize that, if anyone should have time to do such things, it ought to be me, right? I'm a writer, for crying out loud! Isn't that my job?

Going back to connect the dots like that is something most people know they could do. But, like doing twenty pushups or jogging a mile, it seems more trouble than it's worth. Introspection like that does not pay off, and it might just bring up bad things that are better left alone. Still, I am where I am. And every once in a while, I wonder how I got here.

So, let's go back to the beginning, shall we? Forgive me for indulging myself in a little exercise in autobiography. My hope is that this will let you in a little bit on who I am and how I got where I am. If not . . . I'll at least try to make it an interesting story.

Everyone has to grow up somewhere. And—as much as we hate to admit this—where and when and how we grow up affects our understanding of the world.

Me? I grew up easy. I mean, sure we had struggles. What family doesn't? But there's no getting around it: I had it easy.

For the first decade of my life, my family lived in West Monroe, Louisiana, tucked away in the northeast corner of a semi-rural community there. Don't let my urbane sophistication fool you. I learned my way around a tackle box and owned a BB gun before I owned a bicycle. We ate catfish and hushpuppies and turnip greens and black-eyed peas. And we liked it.

My father was the dean of a now-defunct seminary (so there was a fair amount of pressure to know the right answer in Sunday School). He also preached for a small church in the even smaller town of Hale, Louisiana, a place so unremarkable it did not even have its own post office. Go ahead and look it up. I dare you to try to find it on a map.

The accents were so thick. One weekend, we visited another church in nearby southern Arkansas, and my teacher told us that if we weren't good boys and girls, we might end up in "hay-ull." I summoned all the smart-alecky-ness I could for a six-year-old and informed her that I wasn't afraid of going to "hay-ull." After all, my dad preached there most Sundays.

One of the board members of the aforementioned institution where my father was employed gave several faculty members plots of land in a neighborhood called Happy Acres. We lived there—and I am not making this up—on Love Street.

Everyone in my neighborhood went to the same church. Most of the dads worked together. We all went to a Christian school that was started by our parents for us. If it truly takes a village, we certainly were one. Everyone's parents disciplined everyone's kids.

Lest you think I'm wearing rose-colored glasses or enduring a bout of nostalgic rhapsody for a mythical Camelot that never actually existed, I do recognize, looking back with adult eyes, that there were hard times. We weren't rich. We lived in a modest three-bedroom house. We once had an Oldsmobile that broke down and sat in our driveway for a couple of years. We didn't have the money to fix the transmission, and my dad, being as unhandy as he was educated, simply made the payments and got by on one car.

And there were dark times, too. Some sinister things happened in that environment, things that I'm not going to write about. At least, not yet. Maybe one day. When I'm stronger. I mention it lightly here because it's important for you to know. Bad things, things like abuse or neglect, things like violence or assault, whether they are endured or merely observed, these things shape the way we think about the world, ourselves, and our place in the world. They lead us to think and do things we wouldn't otherwise. They force us to come up with defense mechanisms that "work" for us when we're young and trying to survive, but they end up working against us as we get older. And far too often they surface when we least expect or want them to. Tactics that allow us to feel safe in childhood can be dangerous when used as adults.

I've learned that recently.

My sister likes to say that because my father was a leader in the church, we got to see the clowns with their makeup off. We heard the racist jokes. We knew whose marriage was in trouble. We watched people get away with things, sometimes terrible things, and never suffer the consequences because of their status and position in the community. It's easy for a preacher's kid to become cynical.

Still, my parents did their best to protect me from most of the ugly stuff when I was a kid. For example, I had no idea that a casserole was served toward the end of each month because my parents, like so many other parents in the mid-to-late-70s, were struggling to make ends meet. I was blissfully unaware of such things. I believed my mother planned such meals far in advance rather than simply combining bits and pieces of leftovers at the last minute, ghosts of dinners past comingling with rice and cream of mushroom soup.

I thought we occasionally ate breakfast foods for dinner because it was an exotic change of pace. It felt like the kind of thing they must do in France. That being the extent of our family hardships, I'd say, yeah, I had it pretty easy, and, to a large extent, I believe what I believe to this day as a direct result of my early childhood experiences.

LIFE IN THE SUN

Oh, and it got better from there. We eventually moved to the suburbs of Orange County, California. In the early-80s, that pretty much defined having it easy. For five sunny years, we lived the good life in Cypress, California—hometown of Tiger Woods and John Stamos.

Wealthy enough to live there, too poor to own, we rented a bigger-than-we-needed house in a quiet, little neighborhood, walking distance from schools and shopping and parks. Of course, no one walks anywhere in southern California, but we could have—if we'd ever been stuck. My father led a growing, vibrant church filled with young, upwardly mobile suburbanites.

He had this motto he used to repeat all the time: "The best is yet to be!" He said it with so much folksy enthusiasm, I have to admit, it was downright contagious. And, when he got up in front of the congregation each Sunday, he'd declare the first half of Psalm 118:24, "This is the day the LORD has made." Then everyone in church would finish it for him, "Let us rejoice today and be glad." And we would all stand and sing "When the Roll Is Called Up Yonder" loudly enough to shake the rafters.

We canvassed neighborhoods, inviting strangers to visit our church. We hosted youth rallies at the beach. We conducted spectacular Vacation Bible Schools with production values that might make the Artistic Director of your local community theatre green with envy. Every Tuesday night, we took over the local skating rink, forcing them to mix a few bad contemporary Christian songs into the regular playlist of early-80s pop music.

This period, too, had a profound impact on me and the way I view the world. I had this sense growing up that no matter what happened, all would be well. If something of mine got broken, it could be fixed or replaced. There would always be something to eat in the refrigerator. There is a solution to every problem. There will always be something under the tree on Christmas morning. These were assumptions I came to believe in so deeply that I never one time doubted their certainty.

In some ways, it's got even better the older I've grown. I ate more food than I needed last night. I live in a house that's nice. It's not huge. In fact, it's pretty modest by today's standards, but it's still larger than most houses have been for most of world history.

I make money. Sometimes I make a lot of money. Other times I don't make so much, but no one in my family has ever gone to bed hungry. We've never been thrown out of our home. We've managed to pay our bills on time, had a roof over our heads, food on the table, shoes on our feet. My kids have never had to worry about any of this. And I can see this shaping their worldview.

This is important because your worldview shows up in why you vote, what you watch, where you shop, how you drive. Your worldview determines how you talk to yourself and others, how you treat your neighbor, and whether or not you forgive your enemy. Your worldview is demonstrated by your thoughts, feelings, words, and actions.

And your worldview is largely in place long before you ever set foot on a college campus or in the workplace. Your worldview gets set early, before you really have a chance to think critically about such things. And once it's set, it's incredibly resistant to change. This is one of the reasons Jesus told stories. Stories have a way of sneaking past our defenses.

MY NEIGHBOR

In the Gospel of Luke (the single best repository of Jesus's stories in the Bible), we read,

> On one occasion an expert in the law stood up to test Jesus. "Teacher," he asked, "what must I do to inherit eternal life?"
>
> "What is written in the Law?" he replied. "How do you read it?"
>
> He answered: "'Love the Lord your God with all your heart and with all your soul and with all your

> strength and with all your mind'; and, 'Love your neighbor as yourself.'"
>
> "You have answered correctly," Jesus replied. "Do this and you will live."
>
> But he wanted to justify himself, so he asked Jesus, "And who is my neighbor?" (Luke 10:25–29)

Hmmm . . . he wanted to justify himself. Sounds familiar. What do I have to do in order to get eternal life? What can I do to earn it? How can I put God in a position where he owes it to me?

In response to the guy's question, Jesus did what he often did: he told a story. As I mentioned just a minute ago, one of the great things about Jesus's stories is that they sort of force the hearer into identifying with one of the characters. The story Jesus told this man is a little bit of a trap because I inevitably end up identifying with the wrong character.

A man is headed to Jericho—the road there is a bad one, filled with danger and dangerous people. The man gets mugged, and the criminals beat him up pretty badly, throwing him in a ditch barely alive.

Something's got to happen. Someone's got to help him or he will die. Who will show him mercy? A Priest? A Levite? A Samaritan?

I'm guessing a lot of you went to Sunday school. If you did not, I'm guessing you have access to Sunday school or a small group or someplace like that where someone can fill you in on the political tension between the Jewish people and Samaritans. Suffice it to say, they didn't like each other. It was an argument that went all the way back to a civil war between north and south—both groups believing God was firmly (and exclusively) on their side. This was economic, religious, and ethnic prejudice all rolled into one vitriolic ball of hate.

That's the home address of the guy Jesus identifies as the hero of the story. The Samaritan voted the wrong way, worshiped the wrong way, and gave money to the wrong causes. He probably drove the wrong kind of donkey, drank the wrong kind of beer, and didn't recycle.

Whatever it is that drives you nuts, this guy embodied it. That was Jesus's whole point.

Most of us know the story by heart; we've known it since we were children. And most of us know that the moral of the story is this: if someone's in trouble, you should help them out. Anyone in trouble is supposed to be your neighbor.

Right?

Look how the dialog actually ends. Jesus asks, "'Which of these three do you think was a neighbor to the man who fell into the hands of robbers?' The expert in the law replied, 'The one who had mercy on him'" (10:36–37).

Hang on. The neighbor is the one who has mercy. Did you see it, or did you read right over it? My neighbor isn't the one who needs mercy *from* me; my neighbor is the one who shows mercy *to* me.

Well, if I'm not the one who's supposed to show mercy on people who are in trouble, who am I? I'm the one in the ditch. I'm the hopeless one who fell into the hands of the robbers and will most likely die if someone doesn't show mercy on me. That's the point.

All this time, I thought I could earn eternal life if I just knew the right things to do. I want so badly to justify myself. And all along, I'm the helpless, naked one in desperate need of mercy—so desperate, in fact, that I'm willing to accept help from the most unlikely and unsavory sources.

POINTS OF ORIGIN

I grew up somewhere, and so did you. So did the Good Samaritan, and so did the folks listening to Jesus's story. So did the guy who cut you off in traffic the other day. So did the woman who tried to pay the cashier at the grocery store with thirty-seven coupons, an out-of-state check, and no ID.

So did your ex.

So did your abuser.

Everybody has to grow up somewhere, and our point of origin leaves an indelible mark on us. Perhaps the great battle we're all trying to fight is how to make sense of the world when it doesn't fit with our perception of how things ought to be. The "right" answers seem to be so obvious to us, but we keep running into people who refuse to see things our way.

I want to be the hero. Heroes always get the girl. Heroes have bulging muscles and the admiration of the crowd. Heroes are smart and clever and charming and self-effacing. It's easier to be modest when you're stronger and better than everyone else.

But I'm the guy in the ditch. As much as I hate to admit it, I am that guy. I've been beaten up. I've been robbed. I need help. When you're the guy in the ditch, it's hard to be modest. For some reason, you end up trying to present yourself as more "together" than you actually are.

I'm fine. I'll be okay. No, you go on ahead; I'll catch up in a bit.

Here's the truth: I'm broken. Something inside of me is not right. All of the traumatic things that happened to me, and all of the terrible decisions I ever made, all of the lame excuses I've made, and all of the destructive habits I've formed over the past almost five decades of living—they've all worn a rut inside of me. I'm warped in some awful, unavoidable way that I cannot fix by myself.

Until I admit this, I have no chance of getting better. I'll stay there in the ditch, bloody and septic. I may even die there. I am hopeless and helpless until I admit that I am hopeless and helpless. Only then am I in a position to receive mercy.

My name is John Alan Turner, and I am many things. I am a priest. I am a Levite. I am a Samaritan. But mostly, I am the guy in the ditch. Until I admit and deal with that, I'll never be anything more.

CHAPTER TWO

UNMET EXPECTATIONS

I don't want to be me anymore. I'm tired of being me. I'm tired of struggling at forty-seven with the same things I was struggling with at thirty-seven . . . or twenty-seven . . . or seventeen. Tired of fighting the same battles over and over again. Tired of constantly being in process. Tired of being a caterpillar—such a worm as I.

I thought by now I'd have my act together more than I do. I thought I'd be the person God promised to make me into. I'm ready to be a butterfly, to come out of my cocoon, spread my wings, and fly away.

But I'm not there yet. I'm still in the larvae stage. I'm still me.

I was the kid who won all the trivia games at VBS. I could quote the books of the Bible. I knew the names of all twelve apostles, the twelve tribes of Israel, the names of all the judges, the shortest verse in the Bible, the longest chapter, the oldest man, the fruit of the Spirit, the dates when the northern and southern kingdoms were taken into exile. I could walk someone through the plan of salvation before I could ride my bike. I spent Saturday mornings knocking on doors, inviting people to church. I was there Sunday morning, Sunday night, Wednesday night.

I knew that God is good . . . all the time, and all the time . . . God is good.

And I grew up in an environment that made certain promises about the Christian life. I knew that God wanted to turn me into a whole new person, a new creation. I knew he wanted me to have a different kind of life, a better kind of life. I knew that he did not want me to be conformed to the pattern of this world but to be transformed by the renewing of my mind. This renewed mind would enable me to live an exemplary life, doing good deeds that would be seen by men who would, in turn, glorify my Father in heaven.

Yes, I was going to live an exemplary life with a renewed mind, a spotless soul, an energetic spirit, a clean and undivided heart. My crappy life was going to get a major upgrade, and people would take notice. I might even need to be prepared to give an answer when people asked me about the hope I had within me. It would be impossible for them to ignore. I was going to shine like the stars in the heavens, reflecting the glory and goodness of my Creator.

Somehow I got the impression that this process would be quid pro quo. If I did the right things, my life would be good. I wouldn't lose my job if I did all my work as unto the Lord. I wouldn't lose my health if I abstained from smoking and drinking and chewing tobacco and eating foods that had been sacrificed to idols. I wouldn't lose my money if I gave a tenth of my income to my local church. I wouldn't lose my spouse if I loved her as Christ loved the Church, and I wouldn't lose my kids if I brought them up in the fear and admonition of the Lord.

God was some kind of cosmic vending machine. You put the right thing in, and you get what you ask for out. God hears the fervent prayers of a righteous man.

Well . . . I tried. I really did.

I wasn't perfect. I know that. Far from it. But I gave it my best shot. I buffeted my body and beat back the devil. I resisted temptation, gave my life to ministry, and tried to be like Jesus as best I could. I prayed. I fasted. I tithed. I installed filters on my laptop and entered accountability groups. I sought the Lord, expecting him to answer me—to deliver me—to give me the kind of life I wanted. You know the life I'm talking about. A life of rest and peace. A life of purpose and fulfillment. I expected favor with my peers and with my superiors. I expected there to be rivers of living water flowing out of my belly and a hedge of protection always around me.

Instead, I discovered something extremely distressing. In all my struggling and straining to be the person I want to be, my dream-life kept getting farther and farther away. The more I worked, the less progress I had to show for it. The more I tried to manufacture joy, the less joy I had. The harder I pressed for patience, the more elusive patience became. Kids get hurt by people posing as holy men. Church plants fail sometimes—even when you pray really hard. Good men lose their jobs—even when they're not looking at porn in their offices. Marriages come undone. Health sours. Financial problems mount.

Worse, peace and hope begin to fade, and biblically literate people begin to wonder what in tarnation God is up to, if this whole thing is worth it, if the Bible is really true after all. I did the right things, and God just ate all my quarters.

THE ME I WANT TO BE

The me I want to be, the me I thought I would be by now, remains just around the next corner, just over the next horizon, always just out of reach.

And when I allow myself to be honest with myself about this, that's when the voice inside my head starts hammering away at me. "You haven't changed or grown at all, have you? You're the same dirty boy you've always been. God's not doing anything in your life. Why would he? He can't have anything to do with you—just look at you: sinful, shameful, selfish, illegitimate *#@%!. This whole thing is a sham, so just get out there and keep checking those boxes, keep spinning those plates, and keep doing what you can to make yourself at least look better."

So, I put my head down, turn it up a notch, and work harder—checking more boxes, until a few more years go by, and I look up again to find that nothing's changed. I'm still me.

The promises of God aren't working. They're not coming true. I'm doing my part, and God isn't. I feel cheated. I feel duped. I feel angry.

I wrote some of this down in my journal a while back. I was not in my happy place that day, but I was in an honest place. I stared at the words I had scribbled down, barely able to believe my own audacity. What was I saying? Was I saying that I didn't want to live anymore? Was this some kind of suicidal impulse? Was I impugning God's character and doubting his promises? Was I going through some sort of crisis of faith?

I couldn't do that. I was a pastor. I'm a professional Christian, for crying out loud! Professional Christians aren't allowed to think things like this.

But that's one of the great problems in our world: far too many professional Christians aren't buying what they're selling. We haven't experienced the kind of transformation we guarantee others. We're sticking to the script, repeating the party line; but somewhere deep down, many of us suspect it's too good to be true. If anyone is going to get that kind of blessing, it's us, right? Where is my blessing?

I wrote this down in my journal: God is Isaac; I am Esau. The old man gave my blessing to someone else. He doesn't have a blessing left for me.

But I've got to make a living, and this is what I do for a living. So, I go out there and read those promises out loud and encourage people to keep on keeping on. I tell them I know how hard it can be, but you've come too far to only come this far. You don't want to give up and find out later that you were "this close" to your breakthrough! And as the words escape my lips, I want to believe them. I want so desperately for them to be true.

I beg and plead and bargain with God. And the me I thought I would be by now feels one step farther away.

I'm still me. And I don't want to be me anymore.

Actually, that's not entirely true.

I do want to be me. The me I am sometimes. The me I am when I'm in my right mind. The me I am when I'm serving others or helping my daughters through some teenage girl drama. The me I am when one of my clients calls me with a problem they can't figure out, and I help them think it through. The me I am when I'm laughing with my friend Sean as we record a new podcast. The me I am when I'm eating ceviche with my girlfriend Tiffany. The me I am when I'm curious and active, when I'm meditating regularly and working out.

Sometimes I like me. Sometimes I wake up knowing that today is going to matter. Sometimes each moment is like a precious gift, a source of wonder and energy. Sometimes I am able to open up to others, to share what is deepest within me, to listen and respond with openness. Sometimes I'm able to admit my mistakes, repent of my sins, and forgive those who have sinned against me.

It just doesn't happen often enough. I get to that place for a moment, and then I'm back to floundering again. I isolate. I feel uneasy inside. I wallow in pity, and I self-medicate with all sorts of unhealthy things. I am prone to cynicism. I want to believe the worst about people.

Worst of all, I pretend. I pretend none of that is going on. I pretend I'm fine—maybe just a little fatigued that's all. Pretending is exhausting. That's why you feel tired after a first date or a job interview. That's why, when I'm in one of these funks, getting out of bed is hard. I know what's in store for me—a full day of pretending to be someone I'm not. The idea of it makes me want to pull the covers over my head and stay there all day.

That's the me I'm tired of. That's the me I don't want to be anymore. That's the me I am all too often. I'm like the people in Jeremiah 7 who do all this stupid stuff—stuff they know is wrong—but they continue to show up at the Temple rain or shine. I do all these terrible things, but I put on my happy face and sing all the happy-clappy-Jesus-is-my-girlfriend songs. I shake hands, and I clap people on the back.

The people in Jeremiah's day would do all those awful things, but when they came to the Temple, they would declare, "We're safe!" Safe? Safe from what?

You know what safe is? Safe is when you can be who you really are without pretending. Safe is not having to hold your tongue when someone asks you how you're doing. Safe is knowing that you are fully accepted and fully loved regardless of whether you've been a good little Christian this week or not. In that regard, those people were definitely not safe. They were liars. And so am I.

And, I bet, so are you. I bet I'm not the only one who feels like this. I bet I'm not the only guy who feels hollow from time to time. I bet I'm not the only guy who looks at himself in the mirror and wonders what in the world happened to my hair (they say it either turns grey or it turns loose), what happened to my waistline, what happened to my hopes and dreams and plans for this big, bright, amazing life I thought I would have.

THE GAP

As a matter of fact, I know I'm not the only one who feels like that. Everybody I know has a gap between who they currently are and who they thought they'd be by now. Sometimes they're honest with me about that gap and what it does to them. It eats them up from the inside. It hollows them out like a rotting tree. It makes them feel like there's something wrong with them, like maybe they don't have enough faith, or maybe they are sinning in some way they can't figure out. It keeps them up at night. It robs them of their joy and their peace. It keeps them from showing love to and receiving love from others. It makes them feel unworthy.

These people are my people. This is my tribe. We are the ones who aren't done cooking yet, the ones who get hints and glimpses and glimmers of who we can be but cannot seem to get it to stick, the ones who know better but don't know how to get there. Sometimes we want to quit, throw up our hands, raise the white flag, and give up.

In the Bible, we get to read over huge chunks of people's lives in just a few sentences, but we forget that when we read a phrase like "sometime later," this might mean weeks or months of struggle, years or decades of pain and fear and frustration. When I ask people to open up to Genesis 12, all of the long-timers in the room know how Abram's story ends up. We know he and his barren wife eventually have a son. We don't often ponder how hard it must have been for them to have this promise of a child and give it their best shot and have to wait for twenty-four years before the kid shows up.

When we read Genesis 22, we read the words at the beginning of the story that tell us this is just a test. Abraham didn't get to know that. He thought he was going to have to kill his boy. That's an awful three-day trip up that mountain.

I've read the last line of his story, but he has to live it one verse at a time. And that's the tough part. Living one verse at a time.

One. Word. At. A. Time.

Jesus promises that if I come to him, he'll give me rest—but maybe he doesn't mean right this instant. And when he says I'll have rivers of living water gushing out of my innermost being . . . well . . . same thing. It's not happening quickly. When it shows up—if it shows up, it'll be after years of painful struggle. All those good plans he has for me may not come in the foreseeable future, and the deliverance I crave might not even come in this lifetime.

That stinks.

He promised me results; he was unclear on the process and the timeline. It sometimes feels like I've been asked to give birth to myself while he plays the role of midwife.

So, I'm stuck trying to live in the meantime, sitting still while God knocks off all the rough edges and forges my character in the fire and on the anvil. For a long time, I would bring this up in church, and people would stare at me blankly. Then they would tell me about flowers blooming in the spring and butterflies emerging from cocoons and this insane notion that God will not give you more than you can handle. Seriously?

No one wants to talk about the God who dislocated Jacob's hip and makes him walk with a limp for the rest of his life. Or the God who hears Paul's pleadings to remove that thorn in his flesh, but decides he's better off keeping it. That's not the God anyone is looking for. No one wants the God who tells a geriatric couple to make a baby and then waits a quarter of a century before letting them conceive.

No one wants the God who makes unreasonable requests. But, if you're going to take the Bible seriously, you have to admit: that's the only God we have.

I'm forty-seven years old. A woman I know recently went to wake up her boyfriend. He was dead. He was seventy-two. I may have another forty-seven years; I may only have twenty-seven. I'm tired of being me, and it's time to do something about that.

If you're tired of it, too, keep reading.

We're going to figure this out—or die trying.

CHAPTER THREE

DENIAL, DESPAIR, MAGIC

I was flying to San Francisco. I was traveling with my pastor friend, Rick Hazelip, and my Dove-Award-winning musical producer friend, Jeff Sandstrom. We flew into the SFO, rented a car, and drove across the Golden Gate Bridge to Santa Rosa, where we would spend the weekend with a growing, healthy church called New Vintage.

The weather was nearly perfect. The scenery was more than two eyes could take in. The sights, sounds, and tastes were so overwhelming that we found ourselves praying on a near-continuous basis: "Thank you, God, for this!"

The one black eye on our trip, however, came early. As we were getting settled in the hotel, I went out to the rental car to retrieve my briefcase so I could check my email. On my way back into the hotel, I was hurrying to catch the elevator. An older gentleman was holding it for me. I reached into my pocket for my room key, and the keys to the rental car slipped out . . . slid across the floor . . . toward the elevator . . . and . . . (in what seemed like slow motion) down the two-inch gap between the hotel floor and the elevator . . . down the elevator shaft!

The older gentleman and I both watched the keys, following them with our eyes as they slid across the floor and then down the gap. It was almost as if we were hypnotized by them or stunned into disbelief that such large keys could fit into such a tiny space. After they fell and were gone from sight, he looked up at me and said, "That's the most unluckiest thing I ever saw."

Fitting words.

I went straight to the front desk and was told that it's against the law for anyone other than the "elevator people" to go down there, and there's no way they're coming out for this. I did look down the gap with a flashlight later and saw credit cards, earrings, wristwatches. Apparently, this has happened before. The "elevator people" don't come out to look for lost items.

So, the next call was to the rental car company. They sent a locksmith who opened the car (so we could get our other belongs and the rental car contract). But they could not cut a key that would start the engine. It was some new-fangled electronic thing programmed so that when you insert the key into the ignition, the ignition switch asks the key a question. If the key doesn't answer correctly, you can turn on the electricity in the car (radio, air vents, windshield wipers, etc.), but you cannot make the engine turn over.

This was turning into a most unluckiest thing.

The next call was back to the rental car company, who sent a tow-truck. I got to ride all the way back to the airport with the tow driver, a nice man named Mike or Joe or Stan or something like that. We talked about his troubled marriage most of the ride.

Back at the rental car company, I got to endure the "Oh-you're-that-guy-who-lost-the-keys" routine for about twenty minutes. I got to tell the "most unluckiest thing I ever saw" story about five times. "Hey, Louise, you gotta hear this guy's story. I never heard nothing like it before. Go on, Mr. Turner, tell her."

Finally, on my way back to Santa Rosa, the fog had rolled in and was so thick I was across the bridge before I even knew I was on it! I met up with the guys and my sister and brother-in-law for a late dinner (especially for those of us on Eastern Standard Time). But the food we enjoyed and the conversations we had that night were wonderful.

I learned that it's possible to be unlucky and blessed at the same time.

TOW TRUCK TRUTH

One of the things I talked about with the tow truck driver was the idea of happiness. He said his current relationship with his wife (she's not really his wife, but they've been together for a long time and he refers to her as his wife) is frustrating at times. They have a good time together, but she came with baggage in the form of two failed marriages and four kids. He wonders if he's missing out on something by staying with her. He wonders what it would be like to be with a woman who doesn't have that kind of past or responsibilities. He wonders what it would be like to have kids of his own. He was looking for someone to give him permission to get out.

He had talked to his dad, and his dad told him, "Just do whatever makes you happy."

I said, "With all due respect, Stan, that's terrible advice. I'm sure your father's a fine man, and he means well. But you can't just 'do whatever makes you happy.' Life doesn't work like that."

Stan looked at me like I was an alien.

It was quiet, so I continued, "There's got to be something deeper than happy. I'm not very happy right now because of the day I've had. Circumstances change. Someone could run a red light right now (we were on Nineteenth Avenue by this time), and ram into your truck. You wouldn't be happy anymore, right? Happiness allows other people too much control. Happiness isn't internally regulated. It's dependent upon too many other things that are out of my control."

He was nodding his head and seemed to understand what I was saying, so I continued.

"There's such a thing as joy, and joy doesn't come and go based on the circumstances. Joy is often experienced 'in spite of' bad things that happen. A lot of times, I find myself experiencing joy as a result of showing integrity. When I do what I said I was going to do—even though it got hard. When I don't turn away from difficulties. When I keep a promise. When I tell the truth even though it would be easier to lie. Those things bring me joy—in spite of how things turn out. When I know I did the right thing, I can look at myself in the mirror and know."

By this time, we were at the airport and had to say goodbye. I have no way of knowing whether my tow truck driver stayed in his "marriage" or not. But I do know that it's possible to be unlucky and experience joy at the same time.

The problem is, I'm a much better talker than I am a doer. All of those things I said to Mike or Joe or Stan or whatever his name was, I believe them.

Mostly.

But I also know from personal experience how hard it is to live like that. It's hard to celebrate when you feel defeated. It's hard to have integrity when you feel like it too often goes unrewarded. It's hard to endure. It can be hard to tell the truth—especially when the truth isn't particularly flattering to oneself. I live Romans 7. The good that I want to do, I can't seem to do it. And the bad stuff that I swore I would never do again, I can't seem to stop. I'm not sure what the modern vernacular for "Who will rescue me from this body that is subject to death?" would be, but my guts shout that phrase to the skies at least once a week.

ANTIDOTES FOR ANXIETY

And when you get caught doing something monumentally foolish—texting an old flame, getting a DUI, telling a lie to cover your tracks—that's when anxiety can really take over. And that's when life becomes dangerous. Anxiety will kill you if you let it. It will wreck your relationships, your self-esteem, your work, your sense of identity. Anxiety is the enemy of love, joy, peace, patience, kindness, goodness, faithfulness, gentleness, and self-control.

Anxiety is the opposite of the life I want. Saint Paul tells us, "Do not be anxious about anything" (Phil. 4:6). And yet I remain anxious.

Now, when it comes to anxiety, there are two different classes we should consider. There is acute anxiety. This has a specific cause and a finite lifespan. When you get that call from the doctor's office—the one where they say, "Dr. French would like you to come in and discuss the results of your recent test"—well, it's normal to feel a twinge of anxiety in that moment. When your boss starts a conversation with the words, "Our numbers are down, and we're going to have to make some cuts," again, it's perfectly natural to experience some anxiety. You know what the cause is, and you know it's not going to last forever. You can get medical care. You can find a new job. This is acute anxiety.

But then there's chronic anxiety. This is the kind of anxiety that doesn't really have a specific cause, and it doesn't dissipate over time. If anything, it grows stronger. You can actually become addicted to anxiety. Anxiety becomes normal to you. We've all known people like that, people who bring drama with them wherever they go. Ironically, it is these people who are most likely to say, "I hate drama." If there's no drama, rest assured, they'll stir some up. They don't know how to live without a heightened state of anxiety.

What makes anxiety so nefarious is that, in times of heightened anxiety, people are prone to three perspectives on life: Denial, Despair, and Magic.

If you're in denial, you will not acknowledge a problem. "Problem? What problem? I don't have a problem? Maybe you have the problem, and you're just projecting it onto me. Have you ever thought about that, smart guy?"

Despair takes a slightly different approach. It recognizes the problem but denies that there's a solution. "What's the use? It'll never work. We tried that before, and it never got us anywhere."

And that leaves us with Magic. Magic wants a solution that will work immediately, cost us nothing, and alleviate every single problem we have. People who want magic are gullible, easy prey for charlatans and snake-oil salesmen. The Christian publishing industry thrives on this, banking on your congregation's anxiety to prompt them into buying the latest and greatest "40 Days to a Problem-Free Life" curriculum. Somewhere on a shelf out there is the silver bullet.

Personally, I tend to fall into the Magic group. I want an elegant solution. I want to grow up and become mature, attaining to the whole measure of the fullness of Christ. I want that. I really do. I just want it to happen painlessly and quickly. I don't want it to cost me anything. I want it to be easy and convenient. I want a magic potion to drink or an incantation to recite.

Magic allows me to control the process, maybe even manipulate it. Magic is a guarantee that God won't eat my quarters again. When you say, "Open Sesame," it has to open, Sesame. That's what makes magic appealing. With just a wave of my hand or a tap of my magic wand, I can make my character flaws and bad habits disappear. With the right words, spoken in the right order, I can make virtue appear like pulling a rabbit out of a hat.

Last week I was on a cruise ship, and I watched a magician (illusionist, if you're a purist) do some pretty astonishing things. He made a woman's wedding ring disappear and then show up on his keychain that had been in his back pocket the whole time. He made a guy's fifty-dollar bill show up in a box that had been padlocked onstage the entire show. I sat in amazement as these things unfolded before my very eyes, and, in the end, Tiffany and I both asked in unison, "How did he do all of that?"

Of course, we know it wasn't magic. It was sleight of hand. It was misdirection. It was smoke and mirrors. It was all in good fun.

But, boy, if magic were real . . .

Sometimes I pray about things. I know I'm supposed to pray without ceasing, but I'm just being honest. I don't do that. I pray intermittently. I pray a lot of "bottle rocket" prayers—quick, short blasts of prayer fired up in a hurry. Sometimes, I try to make deals with God. If he'll give me this, I'll give him that. That kind of prayers. I'm not proud of it, but it happens.

Sometimes, though, I really pray in earnest. Sometimes I pray earnestly. I remember the first Christmas after the divorce. I was living alone in a house big enough for my entire family. My daughters were with their mother, and there was not a sound in my house. The silence was deafening. I was miserable, and I had it out with God. For nearly two hours, I walked around my house railing at the sky, shaking my fist at the heavens, shouting and cursing and weeping. At one point in time, I caught a glimpse of my reflection and thought, "This must be what the prophets of the Old Testament looked like." My next thought was, "It's also what a lot of the homeless people downtown look like."

There's a fine line between a prophet and a homeless guy.

But I can tell you this with the utmost sincerity: That morning, I did not pray politely, but I did not pray selfishly either. I prayed with a clean conscience. I prayed from my guts. I prayed for good things with good motives and good intentions. I didn't ask God to let me win the lottery or to have a lost weekend at a private beach with a supermodel. I asked for noble things. A good woman to love. A better relationship with my kids. Enough money to pay the bills. Health. Wisdom. Guidance. Growth. Help. Opportunities to utilize the meager gifts I have. A miracle. That's it! A Christmas miracle. It would be perfect. God, please, send me a miracle this year for Christmas.

And then I sat down and listened. I sat down on the stairs in the middle of my house and waited for . . . something. Some answer. Some kind of sign. Something. A wet fleece. A trumpet sound. A still, small voice. Anything.

Instead, I heard nothing. The refrigerator was running. I could hear that. The heat kicked on. I heard that. Nothing more.

God is, without a doubt, the single most frustrating person I have ever met. He is too real for me to live in denial. He is too powerful for me to live in despair. But he is too slow and methodical for me to believe in magic.

On the road to maturity, there are no shortcuts. No secret paths. No hidden portal to transport you from one end to the other. No potions or incantations. No rabbit in a hat. No cards up the sleeve.

No, when it comes to maturity, the only way out is through. Sometimes, when you ask God to help you move the mountain, he gives you a shovel and a wheelbarrow.

CHAPTER FOUR

TRAPPED IN THE CLOSET

Without a doubt, the single silliest thing I have ever watched on television was the urban "hip-hopera" *Trapped in the Closet* by R. Kelly. It was late, I couldn't sleep, and that show was so bad that it was impossible to look away. Like a train wreck. Bad in ways I didn't think possible. What can I say?

Bad like *Plan 9 from Outer Space* meets *Howard the Duck* meets *Santa Claus Conquers the Martians.* So bad it was kind of *Sharknado* good.

For those of you who are unfamiliar with *Trapped in the Closet,* it's a twenty-two-chapter musical opera sung from the point of view of a man who wakes up in the bed of a woman with whom he had sex the previous night. When the woman's husband arrives unexpectedly, the man is forced to hide in a bedroom closet. Hence the title of the song.

Things go from predictable to ridiculous. There are dizzying plot points and twists involving little people and guns and allergies—with cliffhangers at the end of each chapter that virtually force you into watching the next installment. The point of the whole thing is that infidelity can ruin lives and, very often in this world, what goes around comes around.

The reason I bring this up now is because I believe there's another point to R. Kelly's magnum opus. And this is where it moves from silly to sensible. It is this: just about everyone spends time trapped at some point in time or another.

It is, of course, impossible for us to hear those closet words without thinking about LGBTQ people. The phrases "in the closet" and "out of the closet" have become shorthand for people who either refuse to publicly acknowledge their sexual orientation or do so with some measure of pride. "Coming out (of the closet)" is, to some degree, for gay people what being baptized is for Christians—a public declaration of identity.

But, when I say that everyone spends time "in the closet," I simply mean that people hide. It's been our tendency since Eve handed the fruit to Adam back in Genesis 3. We hide as if our lives depend on it. We hide because it's easier to pretend we're something we're not than it is to be honest and run the risk of rejection. We hide because we're afraid.

I know I've logged some time keeping secrets, saying one thing out loud but believing something else in private. I know what it's like to fear for your job or your relationship, to worry that if the other party knew what you really thought, felt, or did, you might lose something that you can't imagine having to replace.

In our current Christian culture, the consequences of confession are often exactly the same as the consequences of being discovered. If you confess an affair, you receive the same treatment as one who is found to be having an affair. Telling someone you've been looking at porn results in the same thing as when someone finds porn on your computer. Why not hide and try to cover things up as long as you can?

And it's not just true of moral failure. It's true of doctrinal drift. I have very good friends who don't believe all of the things they believed when they came out of graduate school. But if they go public with all of that, their alma mater may disown them. They may have their credentials removed. They may lose their jobs. So they hide. They pretend. They avoid those topics in very carefully crafted ways. They are terrified of having someone in their congregation find out what they really believe about the long ending of Mark's Gospel or the historicity of the first eleven chapters of Genesis.

Or women's roles.

Or same-sex marriage.

Or our current president.

Better to pretend. Better to hide.

But that's not healthy. It's certainly not what God wants for us. God wants us to live lives of authenticity, integrity, and courage. This is the only true path to real intimacy—which is what I want most.

What keeps me from living like that, though, is that I'm afraid—sometimes justifiably so—of how people will respond to me. If others really knew the truth about me, about some of the things I believe or some of the things I have done, they might reject me. So, I go on hiding, trapped in a closet of my own making.

The cost of living a fear-filled life is incalculably high. From my own experience, I can tell you that living in fear eats away at your self-esteem and makes you feel hollow. Living in fear causes stagnation instead of growth, and you live with the pain of unrealized potential. Living in fear costs you joy. Living in fear leads to regret as the "what ifs" slowly turn to "what might have beens."

Hiding actually produces the feelings of isolation I'm attempting to stave off by hiding in the first place. I carry deep within my heart the certain knowledge that I can only be loved to the degree I'm accepted. But I can only be accepted to the degree I'm known. If I'm never willing to let others know who I truly am, I'll never be truly accepted, and, worse, I can never be truly loved.

To compound the problem, living in fear is contagious. It's practically an epidemic in our society.

And the one place where there should be no fear should be the church. After all, doesn't perfect love drive out fear?

The church ought to be a place where I can bring stuff into the light, so I can find acceptance and community and healing—for the sins I've committed and the sins that have been committed against me. If I feel shame for things I've done—well, that may be appropriate at times. But I should never feel shame for being a sinner just like everybody else.

We're all sinners by orientation and by action. None of us can fix our sinful orientation. In fact, I'm not even sure I can trust myself to know exactly what's wrong with me—that's how broken I am. I am broken to the point of being disoriented about (and by) my own orientation. The Bible refers to this as a "sin nature," and it says we've all got one. "All have sinned and fall short of the glory of God" (Rom. 3:23).

That sentence wasn't written about the people outside of the Christian community. It was written to insiders about insiders. All means all. It means you. It means your favorite televangelist. It means me. "We all, like sheep, have gone astray" (Isa. 53:6). I don't like hearing that any more than you do, but it's true.

Some of the things I think of as good traits are part of what's messed up inside me. I can't always tell what to keep and what to chuck, so I bring the whole shattered mess to God and ask him to help me, to heal me, to fix me. I know it will be a difficult and painful process. I also know it will involve my cooperating with him by saying no to certain things I want right now and saying yes to certain other things I may not want.

This is how it is with all of us. Christians would be wise to remember this and extend grace and mercy toward all of our fellow-sinners, regardless of their orientation.

One Sunday morning, I was preaching at The Bridge Church just outside of Atlanta, Georgia. We had just moved into our new building, and we used to joke that we had only been able to raise enough money for one bell and one whistle. We knew we couldn't compete with the technology on display at some of the other churches in our area, but we were trying to do our best. We did have two "smart lights" above our main stage, and we were kind of proud of them.

On this particularly Sunday, however, we'd had a round of major thunderstorms sweep through the area, leaving us with only minimal power in our building. We could turn on our work lights, but we weren't even sure we could get the amps up and running in time for worship. The band played an unplugged set, and I got up to speak. I was doing a series called "Slaying the Giants"—dealing with money, sex, and power. This sermon was on the power of sex and sexual sin.

It was a little uncomfortable.

I managed to talk about the sexual sins we commit but also to touch on the fact that there were probably people there who had been sinned against in a sexual manner. I assured everyone that healing was available, but that there is no healing in hiding. We had counselors available to meet and talk with and pray with and for people, but those people would have to make the commitment to step out of hiding.

As I was saying the words one final time, "There is no healing in hiding," the smart lights above the stage suddenly came to life as the power was restored throughout our entire campus. Both lights whirred around in circles, flashing on and off, until they both came to rest, in a perfect pool of light, focused precisely on a woman seated in the third row!

She turned one hundred shades of red, and I said, "Is there something you'd like to confess to us all right now?" Everyone had a very good laugh about it.

But I'll tell you the truth: there are times when I feel exactly what she must have felt. I feel the heat of those lights. I feel the weight of everyone's gaze. I wonder if they can see the sin on me. I know where I've been. I know what I've done. And, as much as I am embarrassed and humiliated, there is a part of me that wants desperately to unburden myself. How healthy, how holy would it be, if we had a place to do that?

If we're ever going to have a chance of being the city set on a hill that Jesus said we are supposed to be, if we're going to shine like stars in the sky, if we're going to fulfill any of the metaphors and descriptions we find in the pages of Scripture to describe the community of faith, we've got to create safe spaces. I don't mean that in the way the phrase is being used on college campuses these days. I don't mean spaces where nothing offensive or challenging is ever spoken. I mean places where people feel safe enough to reveal their brokenness, to share their shameful stuff, to own their dark matter. And to receive not condemnation but compassion, not reprimand but mercy, not dismissal but grace in their time of need.

If you find a place like that, will you tell me where it is? I'll be hiding in the closet until you do.

CHAPTER FIVE

FORGETTING

Immediately after the accident, I felt sore and stiff. I figured it would go away—like if you go to the gym after a long layoff. You get up the next day and work out again, and it gets better. But it didn't get better. I went to see my doctor the next day, and he ordered a series of x-rays. He prescribed a muscle relaxer and some pain medication—Tramadol and Diclofenac.

The pain grew more and more intense. I went to see a physical therapist and a chiropractor. I had an MRI done. And, eventually, a CT scan. I was diagnosed with a concussion after experiencing headaches, vertigo, and the loss of words. I would tell people the same story multiple times. I lost some social skills. I talked too much and too loudly. I behaved irrationally at times. I engaged in risky behavior. I would get dizzy walking the aisles at the grocery store. I was easily confused. And easily agitated. I forgot simple things—appointments, agreements. I began to hear the strange voice of paranoia whispering odd things into my ears. I thought I was losing my mind. I didn't know about the concussion.

When I would drive, I would be overly cautious. And I would constantly check my rearview mirror. I would brace for impact when someone came too close. I would flinch anytime I saw a van behind me.

I was told that I have three bulging discs in my lower back and two in my neck. I experienced pins and needles, tingling in my right foot and calf and in my left hand. It was just half of my left hand, the outside, the ring finger and pinkie. I thought that was weird, but I learned that's the ulnar nerve being pinched by the discs in my neck. I couldn't type very well. My left hand kept missing keys. Or hitting the same key multiple times. That's not good for a writer.

Sometimes it felt like I was wearing a boot full of bees. There was also a burning sensation running down the back of my right leg, consistent with sciatic nerve pain. My physical therapy continued until—you guessed it—my insurance wouldn't pay for any more. I hit my heath insurance deductible in February. Eventually, I had three injections of corticosteroids into my lower back.

I've tried to come off the opioids and have gone to Tylenol 3 with codeine—which doesn't really work. All of that has left me fuzzy headed, not as quick or sharp mentally as I was before the accident, diminished like a retired boxer.

I still have bouts of depression, risky behavior, and the potential to be self-destructive. I have difficulty sleeping, getting to sleep and staying asleep. I get angry much more quickly now. I do stupid things that don't make sense. I push people away. I close up and shut myself off to others. I am darker. Less open.

I have trouble finishing tasks. I am sometimes in so much pain that I cannot concentrate to write, but when I take something for the pain, I'm so loopy I cannot concentrate to write.

I was diagnosed with the flu a while back—the legit, go to the pharmacy and spend $240 on Tamiflu kind of flu. I was also prescribed a prednisone pack. Six days flat on my back and a full round of steroids helped with the pain tremendously. So much so that I thought I had been healed. However, in the past week, the pain in my neck and back has returned. The boot full of bees. The familiar burn near my right hamstring.

It's not as bad as it once was, but it's pretty bad. The chronic pain has led to the depression, and—if I'm being completely honest—some pretty dark thoughts. I sometimes wonder if this is my new normal. Will I be in pain for the rest of my life? Will I struggle with the dark cloud of depression forever? Will I ever be as sharp and focused as I once was?

The damage from the wreck has damaged relationships. It has diminished my libido. It has devastated me financially, as medical bills pile up while work projects remain undone. I have been unable to exercise, so I have gained weight. My energy level is low. I do not feel good about myself. On my good days, I feel like I am about 80 percent of the man I was before the accident. Most days, I feel about 65 percent. I feel like I got robbed of vitality, of life-force.

LIVING WITH MY LOSSES

I could go into greater detail about certain things, but I wanted to write it this way first. I wanted to get the emotion out of it. I know my attorney wanted something she could use as some kind of formula. She says there's some actuarial table out there that considers various inputs, numbers, and factoids and spits out a recommended compensatory amount. I realize this sort of a document does not lend itself to that easily.

But I needed to write it this way. I needed to emote for a bit. No one seems to understand how much of an emotional and psychological toll this has taken on me. Most, having grown weary of hearing me complain, simply say some variation of, "Buck up, Cowboy! We all got pains."

But this is different. This wasn't the slow creep of old age. The normal aches and pains that accompany growing older did not sneak up on me. This was a three-thousand-pound cargo van traveling at forty miles an hour, ramming me from behind and stealing from me the better part of a year of my life with no clear indication of when or if I'll ever return to normal. It destroyed more than my car. In some strange way I cannot quite explain, it destroyed a part of me.

I know the guy who hit me didn't do it on purpose. I know he feels terrible. I don't think he's a bad person. I also know there are people who have been through something like this and came out much worse off than I am now. I can still walk. I can still talk and think. I still have the use of all my limbs. But I'm not me anymore. I'm not whole. I hurt. There's no comfortable way to sit with this.

And I didn't do anything to deserve it. I wasn't drinking. I wasn't texting. I wasn't distracted by the radio. I was sitting still on Peachtree Industrial Boulevard waiting for the car in front of me to move. I don't know if that means someone has to pay. I don't mean to demand my pound of flesh. But maybe. Maybe someone should pay. I don't know how much, but something. Right? Someone should probably pay something that might help me feel closer to whole again. I guess.

I know money won't solve all my problems. But money can help me pay my bills, the bills that got bigger as I took time off work to visit doctors and physical therapists, to lie still in a metal coffin while pictures were taken of my damaged skeleton; bills that piled up while I sat in a stupor, unable to generate a coherent sentence that would travel from my brain, through my hands, and to a page; bills that stacked up as I struggled with self-esteem and headaches and sadness and rage over how much my body has betrayed me.

I will never again be who I was when I was forty-six years old. Time and circumstance have seen to that. Money will not bring that back. But money might just be able to help me regain some modicum of self-respect and dignity and health—the kinds of things one normally cannot put a price tag on.

See, the one thing that I have consistently been asked to bring to the party is my mind. That's my thing. That's what people want. That's what people remark on. I have the kind of mind that remembers things, notices details. I can recall which book that funny anecdote comes from. Mine is the mind that can do the pattern recognition, anticipate what's about to happen, and know how to strategically plan for the future. I understand systems, politics, group dynamics. I can see things from thirty thousand feet that few other people can see.

At least I used to be able to do all of those things. Now . . . I'm diminished.

I was speaking with a friend the other day. She had something similar happen to her several years ago. Back pain and a brain injury. She said, "I used to have a thesaurus in my brain. I had a bench of words nine deep. If I didn't want to use this one, I could pick any of the others at any time. Now, the bench is only about three words deep. I don't have as many to choose from."

That's what I'm dealing with.

And, like I said, I forget things now. Maybe it's just that I'm approaching fifty, but it seemed to happen overnight after the accident in October of 2016. I was the guy who never had to write anything down. I could just remember. Dates. Phone numbers. Shopping lists.

Now I forget what I walked out to my car to get. I forget which story I was going to tell. I forget that I've already told you about that. And I hate it. I am the guy who knows stuff, the guy who remembers stuff. Who I am depends on my ability to remember.

There once was a man named Jimmie, and he suffered from a disease called Korsakoff syndrome. It left him unable to remember anything that happened to him after the age of nineteen. Dr. Oliver Sachs met Jimmie in the 1970s. By this time, Jimmie was in his fifties. But Jimmie believed it was still 1945. Every time they met, Dr. Sachs had to introduce himself as if they were meeting for the first time. Every time Jimmie looked in the mirror, he expected to see his nineteen-year-old face. Imagine his shock and surprise to instead be greeted by his gray-haired reflection.

Who you are depends on your ability to remember.

When the Apostle Paul sat down to write a letter to the church in Corinth, he had heard some negative things about them. There were divisions and factions among them. Rather than gathering to celebrate their unity, they gathered into clusters of haves and have-nots. Instead of remembering the body of Christ, broken for all of us, they were dismembering the Body of Christ.

Paul wants to bring them back to the core of their faith, to its very essence. He writes,

> For I received from the Lord what I also passed on to you: The Lord Jesus, on the night he was betrayed, took bread, and when he had given thanks, he broke it and said, "This is my body, which is for you; do this in remembrance of me." In the same way, after supper he took the cup, saying, "This cup is the new covenant in my blood; do this, whenever you drink it, in remembrance of me." For whenever you eat this bread and drink this cup, you proclaim the Lord's death until he comes. (1 Cor. 11:23–26)

Think about this: Jesus and his closest friends were inseparable for the better part of three full years. They went everywhere together. 24/7/365. They heard him teach. They watched him up close when he healed people. He walked on water. He calmed the storm. He raised the dead. They saw it all happen. They left everything—jobs, family, friends, comfort, everything—to follow him. He completely altered the trajectory of their lives. Nothing would ever be the same.

And, near the end of their time together, he gathered them in a room and essentially said, "Eat this bread. Drink this wine. These will help you remember me."

Was he afraid they were going to forget him?

Well . . . yeah.

I don't think he was worried that they might one day say, "Jesus who?" But he was concerned about their forgetfulness. He knew that who you are depends on your ability to remember.

One time, Joshua led the Israelites across the Jordan River. Once all of them were across, he stopped them, pulled twelve men aside and told them to go make a pile of rocks. Then he said,

> In the future, when your children ask you, "What do these stones mean?" tell them that the flow of the Jordan was cut off before the ark of the covenant of the Lord. When it crossed the Jordan, the waters of the Jordan were cut off. These stones are to be a memorial to the people of Israel forever. (Josh. 4:6–7)

This kind of language is all through the Old Testament: Remember the Sabbath. Remember that you were slaves in Egypt. When you see a rainbow in the sky, remember that I promised I would never again destroy the earth by flood. When you celebrate the Passover, and your children ask you why you're doing that, tell them how your lives were spared by the blood of the lamb. Remember. Remember. Remember.

Christianity is a theology of remembering. Who you are depends on your ability to remember. Why do you think God so often asks us to remember? It's not a trick question. You don't have to have a PhD to answer this one. God asks us to remember because we are so prone to forget. And we have two memory problems.

WE FORGET WHAT WE SHOULD REMEMBER

God delivers the Jewish people from Egypt, and in just a few short days, they're worshiping a golden calf. God didn't slip their minds. They just started to live as though God never saved them, never loved them. I do that, too.

I forget. I forget times and dates and people. I forget events, appointments, and agreements. But I also forget that my bartender is someone for whom Jesus died. I forget that my girlfriend loved me better than anyone ever has, even after I did that unlovable thing. I forget that my daughter is just a teenager who has barely been alive long enough to know who she is, let alone what she wants, let alone how to do it. I forget that we're all fighting some unseen battle and trying to make it through the day as best we can.

When Jesus says, "Remember me," he doesn't just mean call him to mind once a week right after singing a really sad song about his death and eating a cracker. The word he used in his language is the word *anamesis*. We get our word *amnesia* from that. Jesus wants us to avoid a kind of spiritual amnesia, so he gives us these physical, tangible elements, things we can touch and feel and smell and taste. He knows that if we do this his way, something that was once real can become real again.

Maybe you've experienced this. The other day I heard a song. I didn't even hear the entire song—just the chorus of it—"You've lost that lovin' feeling. Whoa that lovin' feeling. Bring back that lovin' feeling 'cause it's gone, gone, gone. Whoa-oh-oh." Instantly, I was sixteen years old, hanging out in the garage with Terry Hobbs and Jeff Hayden. A whole host of memories flooded back, and it was as real as could be.

When I remember the way Jesus intends, the God who delivered Moses from Pharaoh, the God who parted the Red Sea, the God who smashed the walls of Jericho is suddenly present, but the one being delivered is me. The burning bush is here in front of me, and I have to take off my shoes because this becomes holy ground. The God of Abraham, Isaac, and Jacob becomes the God of John and Jason and Jeremy.

I bet if you took the time, you could come up with your own pile of rocks—your own stack of memories of times when God guided you, protected you, blessed you, loved you, healed you. I know I could tell you about the kind women who taught me the words to "Jesus Loves Me" or the gentle men who taught me how true those words are. I could introduce you to the man who baptized me, the guy who acted like the big brother I never had, the friend who is even closer than a brother, the woman who loved me back to life. I have all of this stored in my mind. My problem is I keep forgetting what I'm supposed to remember.

REMEMBERING WHAT SHOULD BE FORGOTTEN

But that's not my only memory problem. I also remember what I'm supposed to forget. I think that may be the worst problem I have. I remember the look in her eyes when she realized I had lied to her. I remember how it felt to get caught red-handed, the scalded feeling inside my chest, the way panic gripped my heart as I knew that the ugly truth was all about to come tumbling out, and I couldn't do a thing about it. I remember every failure, every misstep, every botched attempt. I remember all the times I have screwed up. Like King David, "I know my transgressions, and my sin is always before me" (Ps. 51:3).

I have things lodged in my memory bank, horrible things, things that keep me awake at night, things that I cannot begin to explain away. Sometimes I remember these things and wish I could fly around the world backward like Superman did, reverse time, and undo them. But I cannot. These things cannot be undone, and the memory of them keeps me from remembering the things I'm supposed to remember.

Now, I'm a trained theologian. I've read the books. I've even read most of the footnotes. I know some things. I know that God is not only the world's greatest rememberer, but God is also the world's greatest forgetter. "As far as the east is from the west, so far has he removed our transgressions from us" (Ps. 103:12). I know that verse. I know that my sin is so irrelevant to God's attitude toward me that it's as if God has forgotten it. God has taken on voluntary amnesia for my sake. God, the omniscient, all-seeing, all-knowing being, allows something to escape from his memory.

I know all of this. God remembers what I forget and forgets what I remember. Who you are depends on your ability to remember. I'm not God. I can't forget. But I really wish I could.

CHAPTER SIX

BEING FRIENDS WITH JESUS

I've been a very cerebral person for a very long time. But lately, I've begun to wonder why I feel so emotionally stunted. I think it may be because I've felt the need to explain away my feelings—imposing some sort of rational basis for my emotional ups and downs, rather than simply accepting that I feel this way or that and asking myself probing questions about it.

So, here's what I've been working on: Instead of pretending to feel okay—and explaining to the people around me why I might come across as if I'm not feeling okay—I'm trying to let myself feel what I'm feeling, even if I'm not feeling particularly chipper at the moment. I hope that this will allow me to discover what I need to do in order to move past a not-so-okay feeling.

I've grown weary of pretending to be perfect. I'm going to let myself be human without offering an apology. I'm not perfect. I'm tired of hiding that. All that pretending has ever done is damage my relationships with the people who matter most to me.

Of course, there are times when it makes sense to explain oneself. Someone may have misunderstood something. I may hurt someone accidentally. Explaining my actions (and the intent behind my actions) may bring clarity to confusion at times. The vast majority of the time, however, the only person who needs an explanation about me is me—so that I can figure out what's going on inside of me and work through it.

I can't control what other people think of me, but I'm learning that if I can accept myself in this moment, I might discover what I need to do in order to actually feel better—instead of just trying to look better.

Having difficult feelings does not justify making bad choices, though. This is something I struggle with a lot. I've made big improvements over the past few years, but I still have a tendency—especially when I feel overwhelmed by fear or loneliness or stress or anything else that hurts—to do something monumentally foolish.

I'm getting to the place where I can just sit in the middle of my emotions. I know that's the grown-up thing to do. But sometimes, when I feel particularly powerless, I astonish myself with my own stupidity.

I did that recently. I was asked about something from my past—a part of the dark matter of my life that I prefer to keep locked in the basement. It wasn't a confrontation; it was a question. And I was given assurances that what is in the past is in the past. That experience may have reflected who I was at the time, but that doesn't necessarily mean it defines who I am today. I was told it was safe to talk about it.

But I couldn't. Or I wouldn't. I was seized with fear—fear of rejection, fear of judgment, fear of vulnerability, fear of appearing weak. So, I lied. I looked someone in the eye, and I lied. Someone I love and admire and respect.

When it all came tumbling out, when I could no longer live with deceiving this person, I realized that I had only made things worse. I had brought my dark matter out from the past into the present. That's not a terrible thing, but I had demonstrated that dark matter is still being generated in my life. I had shown myself to be a person who is not always completely trustworthy, a person who is willing to lie in order to make myself look better than I actually am.

All because I let my negative feelings drive me to do something destructive.

Of course, I apologized to this person, and we'll see how the relationship goes from here; but as I sit writing this, it occurs to me that I don't just owe *her* an apology. I think I need to apologize to myself. I owe myself an apology for allowing my fear and insecurity to drive me to do something hurtful and harmful and for beating myself up instead of learning from the experience and moving forward.

That's what I think a good apology is supposed to do: allow us to move forward. So, today I apologize to myself with no excuses and no justifications. I used bad judgment. It's humbling to admit that. I expect more from myself, but as you have probably figured out by now, I am a work in progress.

I cannot change what I have already done, but, if I can be honest with myself, I can learn and grow and continue moving forward. And the path forward begins with trying to figure out how to be secure in who I am and where I am. Seems like a good place to begin that journey might be with what Jesus thinks about me.

JESUS AND ME

A few years ago, a guy named Will Briggs wrote in to my blog and asked me to list five things I dig about Jesus.

Of course, I could list hundreds of things, but he only asked for five. He did not say they had to be the five *main* things I like about Jesus or the five *most important* things or the five *most theologically profound* things. He just asked for five things.

Should be simple enough, right? I mean . . . I'm a writer, and I write and talk about Jesus all the time.

It was, without a doubt, the hardest writing assignment I've ever undertaken.

As I sat there, staring at my computer screen, ideas and thoughts swirled around my mind until they all just evaporated. This is the stuff writer's block is made of.

Eventually, I settled on a list.

The first thing I dig about Jesus is that he had a sense of humor. He told jokes and funny stories and gave his friends nicknames. He got invited to parties (and I'm not talking about church potlucks in the fellowship hall). Sailors and hookers liked to hang out with him. Sailors and hookers don't tend to hang out with people who can't take a joke or tell a joke or laugh at one. They tend to avoid people who are prudish and serious all the time. There must have been something about Jesus that put them at ease, made them feel comfortable. I bet it was his sense of humor.

The second thing I dig about Jesus is that he is one of the all-time greatest storytellers (maybe *THE* all-time greatest). I can sit and read Jesus's stories for hours on end, picking them apart, noticing new details each time. He gave just enough information not to spoil things. He knew how to wait for the big reveal at the end. Sometimes his stories didn't really have an ending, leaving the audience to draw their own conclusions. He was just brilliant.

I love storytellers. Garrison Keillor. Clyde Edgerton. Marilynne Robinson. Ferrol Sams. Edwin Friedman. Shonda Rhimes. Ira Glass. These are some of the great storytellers of recent times. Maya Angelou. Gabriel García Márquez. Ernest

Hemingway. Mark Twain. Charles Dickens. Shakespeare. These are some of the great storytellers of all time.

But none of them could tell a story the way Jesus did. His stories get under my skin. They have a way of drawing people in. We find ourselves relating to one of the characters in the story, wondering what's going to happen next, how it's all going to turn out.

I understand that there's an appropriate time for didactic, right-brain, bullet-list, fill-in-the-blank kind of teaching. But I lament the fact that more preachers and teachers in our churches aren't good storytellers. You don't have to be particularly smart or sophisticated to understand a story.

Sometimes Jesus used his stories to help people who wanted to understand. Sometimes he used stories to hide his real meaning from people who were just looking for a fight. Sometimes his stories worked like time bombs or time-release medicine. It wasn't until people were on their way home that light bulbs came on and they realized, "Hey! That story was about me!"

The third thing I dig about Jesus is that he was smart. Maybe that's an understatement. Jesus was absolutely brilliant. The stories he told, the humor he used, the questions he asked, the answers he gave, the plans he made all speak of a man who had a deep understanding of the human psyche and of the ways this world works. He knew how to do things other people couldn't do. He said things so deep and yet so pithy and quotable that he was clearly thinking on a different plane than most people.

Jesus was smart, the smartest man who ever lived.

But, Jesus never used his intelligence to make people feel inferior. Well . . . there was the one time he confounded the Pharisees and teachers of the Law by asking them about John the Baptist. But other than that, he used his smartness to help people and not to make people think about what a smart guy he was.

I like to think that I'm a smart guy. But I often find myself using my intellect as a weapon. I use it sometimes to control people and keep them at bay. The smartest guy in the class isn't always the most popular guy in the class. But Jesus was both.

The fourth thing I dig about Jesus is that he thought big.

Jesus didn't say, "Just tell a few people about this—your best friend or a coworker." He didn't just talk about winning one poor soul or putting in a good word for him. Nope. He said, "Tell the whole world. In fact, go out there into the wide world and be witnesses about this."

Jesus didn't just say, "I'll improve your quality of life. I'll make things a little better for you." No way. He said, "I've come to bring you abundant life, life running out your ears, life that will never end."

Jesus thought on a global scale. He wanted the entire population in on this deal he was making. He called it "eternal life." He promised not just quantity of life, but a whole new quality of life too. He promised with a description of heaven that surpasses anything we can describe in words. He assured us that he will never abandon us and that our lives will be filled with purpose and meaning.

Jesus wasn't content with mediocre dreams and lukewarm promises. He thought big and dreamed big and promised big, and I like that about him.

The final thing I listed for my friend Will was this: Jesus likes me.

That one's the hardest one to accept. I can deal with the idea that Jesus loves me. He kind of has to, right? He's God, and God is love and all. But I sometimes have to battle the notion that Jesus might be loving me through gritted teeth—like he really wishes he could whack me a good one, but he can't because he has to love me.

But Jesus told his disciples an amazing thing once: he didn't think of them as his servants; instead he thought of them as his friends (John 15:15). Friends? Really?

But see, I know where I've been, and I know what I've done. It's not always easy to like me or to love me (just ask Tiffany!). It's difficult sometimes to think that Jesus doesn't just put up with me from some sense of covenantal obligation. He doesn't just want to order me around. He actually likes me, likes spending time with me, likes talking with me. He comes looking for me when I go into hiding.

Jesus calls me his friend. He likes to spend time having lunch or dinner with me, just talking about stuff.

Jesus likes me; he really likes me!

I BELIEVE

For the record, I believe Jesus Christ is the Son of the living God, coequal with the Father. I believe he lived a sinless life, teaching people the true potential of a human life surrendered to the Spirit of God and offering himself as the perfect sacrifice for the sins of all humanity by dying on a cross. I believe he became alive again after being dead for three days to demonstrate God's power over sin and death. I believe he's the head of the church and the only way to God and eternal life. I believe he went to heaven and now sits at the right hand of his Father until the time he will return to judge the earth as King of kings and Lord of lords.

If you want me to give you some Bible verses to back up all of these beliefs, there are loads. Here are some for starters: Isaiah 9:6; Matthew 1:22–23; John 1:1–5; 14:6–30; Acts 1:9–11; Romans 1:3–4; 1 Corinthians 15:3–4; 1 Timothy 6:14–15; Titus 2:13; Hebrews 4:14–15.

I believe humans are made in the image of God to enjoy fellowship with him and with other people. I believe humanity is the supreme object of God's creation and his love. I also believe that, although humans have tremendous potential for good, we are marred by an attitude of disobedience toward God called sin. This attitude separates us from God and renders us incapable of regaining a right relationship with him through our own effort alone. We can only reach our highest potential by being reconciled to him.

I believe salvation is being right with God. It means having your sins forgiven rather than punished. It means that God's Spirit lives within you, helping you become a real person. It means you will enjoy the presence of God forever after you die. Salvation is God's free gift to everyone who puts his or her faith in Jesus.

I believe people can never make up for their sins by self-improvement or doing good deeds. Only by trusting in Jesus Christ as God's offer of forgiveness can a person be saved from sin's penalty, which is death. The Bible says we are saved by grace through faith.

And here's where I get to something really, really important.

Grace is free. Absolutely free, I tell ya! Free, as in no strings attached, no price tag, no cost to you whatsoever. Complimentary. Gratis.

Salvation involves a complete trust in Christ's completed work. You get saved; you don't save yourself. Couldn't even if you wanted to. Couldn't even if you tried. The only way to be saved is to surrender to it. There's only one category of people in the Bible who receive grace and that is the humble. You get it when you stop trying to earn it and allow someone else to give it to you.

That's salvation.

Repentance is a different thing altogether. Repentance is the changing of your mind about who Christ is and of your general attitude toward sin—namely, deciding that sin is bad and you don't like it anymore because of what it does to you and to your relationships. This change of mind will necessarily bring about a change in behavior, but you can't know what parts of your behavior must change until you're a Christian. Moreover, you can't say for sure when the Holy Spirit will bring about these changes. Your job is just to submit to his leading.

It is this understanding that allows me to say that people who disagree with me over issues of faith and morality also have a legitimate relationship with God. They may be saved. They may be Christians—even if they continue to sin. Because God refuses to give up on us when we make a mistake; the Holy Spirit refuses to leave us when we fail.

God knows I fail and I continue to sin! Every Christian I know fails and continues to sin (especially the professional ones). We're all growing in our understanding of what it means to be like Jesus. The Holy Spirit works on his own timeline, revealing which portions of my lifestyle must be changed or abandoned in order to continue the process of maturity. The abandoning of all sins requires a life-long and sometimes difficult process called sanctification.

I believe the process of sanctification takes place in the context of a growing relationship that looks less like a student-teacher relationship and more like what we'd call a friendship.

Friends of Jesus

Jesus was a teacher, a rabbi. He was more than that, of course, but he certainly wasn't less than that. And to the vast majority of people who knew him in his lifetime, that's precisely what they thought of first when they thought of him.

Like other rabbis of his time, Jesus had disciples. But Jesus was different. Typically, a rabbi would allow a student to approach him about becoming a follower. The rabbi might ask the would-be disciple a few questions to see if that young man was serious about learning. Once approved, the disciple would follow his rabbi everywhere, hoping not only to learn from his teacher but also to actually become more like his teacher.

Jesus, however, reversed this set-up. He was proactive in seeking out his disciples. He didn't wait for them to come to him; he went to them, calling them out of their workplaces to a lifestyle of following and learning and becoming. Mark's Gospel tells us that he settled on twelve guys who would be his closest followers, and Mark tells us what Jesus's primary educational strategy was.

The plan was that they would just "be with him"—just hang out with him, go where he went, watch, listen, ask, discuss, learn, and then, under his watchful eye and careful tutelage, begin doing the same kinds of things he had done (cf. Mark 3:13–15).

Some amazing things happened over the next three years. Sick people were healed. Dead people were raised. Women and children were elevated and dignified. Religious people were confounded. Corrupt people were exposed.

But something else happened. Over time, as Jesus and his followers hung out, their relationship changed. By the end of his life, Jesus didn't just think of them as his servants or his students.

They had become his friends.

He was still their rabbi, and there was still much for them to learn from him. He was their Lord, their Master, and he would become their Savior in a matter of hours. But on the last night before his death, he gathered them all in a rented room and told them, "You guys are my friends now, and there's no greater way of showing you how much you mean to me than by my making the ultimate sacrifice for you."

Jesus wasn't dying as a war hero or a religious martyr. He wasn't laying down his life for his followers or students or witnesses or servants. This wasn't just a theological event staged to satisfy some mysterious part of God's nature. This was a personal expression of the deep love Jesus felt for his friends.

Jesus is many things, and talking about being friends with him brings up some angst in some folks—including me. Jesus is God, and, as such, we are to worship and submit to him.

But one of the distinctive things about Christianity, something that separates Christians from, say, Muslims, is that we believe our God came near. He's not just way out there, totally "other," beyond the azure blue concealed from human sight. He's close. He has willingly drawn near to us. He has called us to be more than servants; he has called us to be friends.

A Savior is someone you need.

A King is someone you respect.

A Master is someone you obey.

Jesus is all of these things. But he's more. He's a friend.

And a friend is someone you know. That's the real difference. And it makes all the difference in the world.

CHAPTER SEVEN

ACTIVE STILLNESS

It's been nearly nine months now since my accident, and I'm frustrated. I thought I was getting better, but recently things have taken several steps back. It's not just the physical part of this that bothers me; it's that the physical stuff has taken a toll on me mentally and emotionally. I'm at a bit of a loss to know how best to move forward again.

I have a suspicion that the answer involves being still. When I had the flu, I had to be still for six days. Flat on my back. It was the best I've felt since the accident. It can't be a coincidence, right? Stillness somehow is connected to getting better. The problem is that I'm still grappling with understanding what exactly stillness is.

Of course, you're not naïve. You know I'm talking about more than physical stillness, don't you? And you know I'm talking about more than my physical ailments. I'm also talking about this whole theme of being transformed, of being changed into the person I thought I'd be by now.

I think maybe I wasn't properly prepared for this journey. We strike out blindly, confident that we'll be guided in the right direction, to the right people. We somehow are convinced that it'll all just work itself out. We may even be prepared for a circuitous path and a few U-turns along the way. But do we know what we're really looking for? Do we even know what we're looking at?

WHAT DO YOU SEE?

There's a long story in John 9 that begins with Jesus meeting an adult—a man who, we later hear his parents say, is "of age"—but this man has been blind from birth, from day one. He's spent countless hours begging for money in the same place day after day. People walk past him all the time without even noticing him. They don't even know for certain what he looks like. It's easy to do that—to walk past the same people in the same places day after day and never really see them. Most of us do it all the time.

We don't just do it with people, either. We read over the same Bible verses again and again and miss the message that is only glaringly obvious after it's pointed out to us by someone else. We can drive through rolling hills or awe-inspiring sunsets, trees and grass and blue sky, rock formations and cloud banks and moving water, and miss it all. We have a way of becoming immune to the beauty of creation, the truth of God, the goodness of life, the needs of the people all around us.

We have a way of seeing without seeing. We look past life in all its fullness—all the joy and sorrow—all the mystery and comedy and tragedy that are so close we could reach out and touch them. If we would only open our eyes and see!

Life wasn't that way for Jesus. He saw. He noticed. He was frequently busy, of course. And he must have been burdened at times with the weight of his assignment. We would understand if Jesus was too preoccupied with other things to notice one blind beggar.

And yet . . . over and over in the Gospels, it seems that noticing people was the primary thing Jesus was preoccupied with.

Part of honoring God is doing what he says. Perhaps it mostly comes down to seeing just as Jesus does.

I have a sneaking suspicion that if I could see as he sees, I would be more likely to do as he says, and things inside of me would begin to change.

I DON'T KNOW

Two major themes run through this story. The first is, of course, the idea of sight and blindness. The man born blind can now see; the Pharisees claim to see, but they are truly blind. Jesus sums up his mission in verse 39 by saying, "For judgment I have come into this world, so that the blind will see and those who see will become blind."

Two verses later he says, "If you were blind, you would not be guilty of sin; but now that you claim you can see, your guilt remains" (v. 41).

But there's another theme: the one called "I don't know." That phrase appears three times in John 9. In verse 12, the Pharisees want to know where the man who healed the blind man went. The blind man's response is, "I don't know."

Later, the Pharisees question the blind man's parents and want to know how it is that he can suddenly see. Their response is, "We don't know" (v. 21). And eventually, the Pharisees try to discredit Jesus to the man he has healed by saying, "We know this man is a sinner." The blind man's response is again, "Whether he is a sinner or not, I don't know. One thing I do know. I was blind but now I see!" (v. 25).

Sometimes, it's important for us to remember that we're not called to be scholars and systematic theologians (not that there's anything wrong with scholars and/or systematic theologians). We're not called to have all the answers and know all the finer points of Christian doctrine. We're simply called to be witnesses—people who observe and share what God has done and is doing.

I have a reputation for knowing lots of information about God. I can walk a person through the eleven major divisions of systematic theology. I can break down philosophical and theological arguments from Augustine to Freud. I'm conversant in Lewis and Luther, Schaeffer and Wright.

But there's so much I don't know. Recently, I caught myself beginning every single prayer with that phase, "Dear God, I don't know . . ."

I don't know what I'm supposed to do next.

I don't know how I'm going to provide for my kids.

I don't know how to love Tiffany well.

I don't know where God wants me.

I don't know what's going on in the world, in the church, in my relationships, in my own heart sometimes.

What is God up to? How is God going to deliver me this time? When will things become clear again?

I don't know. I don't know. I don't know.

That's disconcerting to say out loud. I'm the kind of guy who likes to know. Not knowing keeps me awake at night. Not knowing kills my appetite and gives me the heebie-jeebies.

I'm trying to learn how to rest in not knowing—to take comfort in the fact that the One I pursue and am pursued by knows. And when everything around me seems confusing or unclear, I can at least say: "One thing I do know. I was blind but now I see!"

But I have big questions, big problems that will require big answers. And, as I've said before, I want a magic wand or an incantation that will make it all better right now. More than that, I am coming to believe that answers alone will not suffice. I need abilities. Information won't be enough. I need skills. And skills usually take time.

THE SKILL OF BEING STILL

Through the psalmist, God told the nations at war with his people, "Be still, and know that I am God" (Ps. 46:10). I do not want to take this verse out of context and make it apply broadly to my life. In its original context, God was telling the pagan nations to lay down their swords and acknowledge him as the one true God. Get with the program, or you'll be sorry.

I know the context; don't call the hermeneutical police on me.

But I also know this: I am one of God's people, and I am frequently at war with myself. I know for sure that I stand in the way of much of God's plan for my life—at least the parts of his plan that I can figure out. So, maybe the verse has something to say to me after all.

Cease striving! Quit the battlefield! Retreat! Be still!

But I don't want to be still. I want to get busy. I want to prove that I'm not lazy. I want to show people how hard I'm working. In fact, I get myself into trouble sometimes by taking on too much, working on too many projects at the same time. So many, in fact, that I don't always finish them before moving on to the next adventure. It's a long-standing pattern, and, as counterproductive as it is, I'm comfortable with it.

The accident should have brought all of that to a grinding halt. Instead, I was determined to push through it. I continued traveling. I took on more writing projects. I kept up with the podcast. I'm not sure what in the world I was thinking.

I'm trying to learn how to be still now. This isn't the kind of thing one achieves through daily meditation, which I practice. Meditation helps, but it's more than that. It's also not about being inactive. That just makes me stiff and sore. The kind of stillness I need, the stillness required to come to terms with my not knowing, involves stilling myself, stilling my will, being open to guidance from the Spirit. It's a deliberate act of letting go of my personal agendas, intentions, attachments, and desires.

This is scary stuff.

For someone who is self-employed and likes to be on the move, this is incredibly uncomfortable. But as long as I think I have the answers, or as long as I think I can find the answers if I just look hard enough, I'm only creating resistance. I'm merely allowing fear to fuel me. I'll be sabotaging my own progress and forcing myself to repeat the lesson over and over.

It is only when I can still myself that I can focus myself and concentrate on the things that matter most. Unstilled, I am distracted. I am prone to give in to short-term fixes, surrendering what I want most to what I want now. Insight comes when I am still. It's the only way for me to see things as they truly are, to observe and discern a path forward. In stillness, things become obvious that would never occur to me when I'm busy trying to solve everything.

I've spent too much time settling for a solution to the immediate problems that vex me. Stillness offers the chance to develop skills I'll need next time, the ability to concentrate and view the present problem in light of my overarching sense of purpose, meaning, and direction.

I am where I am. I cannot be somewhere other than here. I am who I am. I cannot be otherwise. I may dream or think or wish that I could be better than I am, in a better place, with greater abilities and powers and so forth. But I am not there right now. Until I acknowledge that, until I see where I am and who I am right now—warts and all—I cannot find the way to be where I want to be or who I am meant to be. I'll never have the means to get there. Stillness is showing me that. Stillness is giving me the fundamental qualities I need for this journey. Concentration. Discernment. Patience. Perseverance. Faith. Compassion. Forgiveness. These are all essential if I'm going to get from where I am (and who I am) to where I want to be (and who I want to be).

When I think too much about the fact that I'm not yet there, I become desperate and needy. I need the answers right now. I'll do anything. I go through all the possible answers that I can think of. Maybe the problem is psychological. Maybe it's physical. Maybe it's medical. Maybe it's philosophical. Maybe it's spiritual. I run through all of the possibilities, and my fear drives me to do foolish things. My actions are full of sound and fury, yet they signify nothing—at least nothing that will accomplish anything of lasting merit. Being active gives me the illusion of productivity; being still is the last thing I want to do.

But very little of the stuff that drives me to despair requires immediate action. More and more, I find that my first step is to be still—even if it's just for a few minutes. Stop trying to answer the question. Discern and acknowledge what I really want. That's a hard thing to do. I don't always want what I say I want. Sometimes I say I want something, but that's just because it's what I think I'm supposed to want.

Being still allows me to be honest with myself, which is vitally important. Liars never heal. I've got to stop lying, and that starts when I stop lying to myself.

Sometimes, if I'm being honest, I don't really want my problem solved. I want a resolution that will give me my preferred outcome and relieve the pain I am feeling. So, I plot and scheme.

The desired outcome is more important to me than discovering a truth about myself. When I get still, I can get past negotiations like these. I can face difficulty. I can just observe some things about myself—even if they are unflattering. I can confront my internal conflicts.

But stillness cannot be approached as a means to an end. Stillness will lead to transformation, but only if I seek stillness for stillness's sake. It will also lead to trust—trust in my own redeemed goodness, trust in the Spirit at work within me, trust in the finished work of Christ for me, trust in the Father who is always working for my benefit.

Stillness is the answer. Stillness is not the pathway to the answer. Stillness is the answer.

Oddly enough, I must summon the strength to still me or I will always remain still me.

CHAPTER EIGHT

DOING THE WORK

August had been miserable in Columbia, Maryland. Hot and humid are even more difficult to deal with when you're dirt poor and living in a one thousand-square-foot apartment. September wasn't much better. Indian summer stretched through the month, and our electric bill (from running the air conditioner 24/7) went through the roof. My wife was a trooper through her first pregnancy. Didn't complain much until right at the end. Then she decided, "I've made it this far. From now on, I'm getting what I want." It was ninety degrees outside and about sixty in our apartment. There could have been a thunderstorm in our doorway!

Making the month especially . . . uh . . . interesting was the fact that my mother decided to come out and stay with us until the baby was born. She was helping . . . sort of.

My father juggled his schedule so he could fly out the day after the due date. He spent an entire week twiddling his thumbs, reading all my books, and jumping every time Jill sneezed. Eventually, she started hiding in the back bedroom. She just got tired of being stared at. Then he left disappointed—no baby.

One Sunday morning we were driving home after church, and my mother ordered me to stop at a produce stand. She bought peppers of every variety and turned them into the hottest salsa she's ever made. Some old wives' tale. We ate salsa until we cried. We went for walks. We did all the things grandmas say will make the baby come out.

No baby.

We blew past the due date. Then we lapped it. Finally, our doctor told us to schedule a time to come in and be induced. We were told to come in late at night. That way we could sleep while they were setting everything up, wake up the next morning well-rested, and have us a baby.

So, after our Tuesday night Bible study, we watched Emeril, packed our bags, waved goodbye to my mother, stopped at the grocery store for snacks, and headed to the hospital. On the way there, Jill had indigestion or Braxton-Hicks contractions or something. The funny thing is . . . they were fourteen minutes apart.

It wasn't until we were sitting in the waiting room filling out forms that I realized she was in labor. There would be no sleep that night . . . or the next.

The best things in life make you wait for what seems like an eternity. You get all excited, mark the date on the calendar in red, and then wait while the days crawl by. You go about your regular activities, but they don't seem to have as much meaning.

In fact, as I look back, I don't remember anything substantial happening—even though I was serving a church and continued my teaching schedule. I know I must have spent time studying and meeting with people. But I can't remember any of that. The only thing I remember is waking up every morning and wondering, "Will it be today?" I remember thinking the same thing every time my cell phone went off during those ten overdue days: "Is it time?"

Every day was filled with hope and expectation and disappointment and more hope. We knew it wouldn't be long, and even though it was longer than we expected, we never lost hope.

Eventually, she ran out of water in there. Lingered and swam and rolled over until there was nothing left in there but her. And she still wouldn't come out. The doctors told us it would be soon. They lied. Jill struggled and suffered and waited too long for the really good pain stuff. I tried my best to keep her distracted, playing Yo-Yo Ma cello music softly in the background, reminding Jill to breathe, and cracking inappropriate jokes at appropriate times.

We laughed a lot and kept the doctors generally confused. But that baby wouldn't budge. Then, after what seemed like an eternity, everyone got in a great big hurry. Her heartbeat was growing faint. The doctor looked scared, and I readied myself for the possibility that I might not get to see her after all.

Suddenly, we were whisked upstairs into an operating room. I had scrubs on, and they were cutting my wife wide open—going in after our little girl who will forever be remembered by the scar she made on her way out. She still prefers to do things in her own sweet time.

I remember holding her for the first time. I didn't have words. Sometimes I still don't. She had a big ridge on her head from where she was stuck. Bobby McFerrin's song "Common Threads" seemed to be playing in the background—or maybe it was just in my head.

NORMAL GROWTH

It all seems like a faraway memory of a dream now. Everything was slow and fast all at the same time. I had no idea what I was in for. You blink, and she's five. You blink again, and she's got a driver's license. Time does not slow down. If anything, it speeds up.

When she was born, she weighed eight pounds and six ounces. That's not enough to qualify as ginormous, but it was pretty big. She lost some weight right at the beginning, but she put it back on. By the time she had her first birthday, she weighed a little more than twenty pounds—more than double her birthweight. Thank God, she stopped! If she'd kept up that pace, she'd weigh more than a million pounds by now!

My middle daughter, meanwhile, came right on schedule—still likes to be prompt wherever she goes. She weighed in at about seven-and-a-half pounds. Not as long and lean as her sister, but no real trouble at all with her delivery.

No, the problem with Eliza came later—about six months later to be precise. She started losing weight. Couldn't keep food in her system long enough to pull the nutrition out of it. She fell off the growth chart. By the time she turned one, the doctor wrote three letters on her chart: FTT—Failure To Thrive.

We took Eliza to a doctor who told us she had thrombocytopenia—which is bad, potentially lethal. It's sometimes considered a precursor to leukemia. Turned out there was a mix-up with her blood in the lab. The blood sample was hemolyzed, and it gave off a false positive. In the end, we were told that we'd been poisoning her for six months with soy milk. So, no rare blood disease; just the worst parents in the world!

She was unbelievably advanced verbally. By the time she was two, she spoke like a three-year-old but still looked like a one-year-old. It really confused a lot of folks!

We put her on a special diet, and eventually she caught up with her peers. She's normal sized now. To look at her today, you'd never know she had a problem. But I remember how frightening the whole ordeal was—and how I would have done whatever I had to do, spent whatever money I had to spend, buy whatever nutritional supplement I had to buy, to get her healthy again.

It's odd that when a child stops growing, we freak out, but when a Christian stops growing, we think it's no big deal. In fact, we're kind of surprised when a Christian does grow—even if it's just a little. Growth is supposed to be normal.

I used to do a thing with my daughters when they were small. I'd squeeze them super tight and command them to stop growing. "Do not grow anymore. This is as big as you are allowed to get. No bigger!"

They would giggle and wiggle and squeal and shout, "Daddy, I can't help it! I have to get big, big, big!" Growth is supposed to be normal.

TESTS: PASSING OR FLUNKING?

I took a test recently. My neuropsychologist administered it to test my intelligence and see if I have any residual brain damage from the accident. I do, so I've got that going for me. Next time someone asks me, "What's wrong with you?" I'm going to reply, "I've got brain damage."

Anyway, I took a test. How long has it been since you took a test? Maybe at the DMV. Maybe it was your vision test. Maybe a cholesterol test. Have you ever taken a test for how well you're doing in terms of your life with God? How much like Jesus you're becoming? What would such a test even look like?

Some Christians seem to think that spiritual maturity amounts to growing in your ability to really annoy the people around you with your smug self-righteousness. Others think it means growing in the number of church-related activities they are involved in. Some act as if it's nothing more than time spent on a church campus.

Or Bible knowledge. The more mature you are, the more Bible verses you know. They seem to forget the fact that the Pharisees did all of that, and they're the bad guys in the Gospels.

Saint Paul says there are characteristics that are relatively easy to spot in someone who is led by the Spirit of God. Love. Joy. Peace. Patience. Kindness. Goodness. Faithfulness. Gentleness. Self-control. This is the center of the target.

Why not take a moment right now and write those words down somewhere and give yourself a grade? Start with love. How loving are you? Would you give yourself an A in loving? How easy to love are you? Would you give yourself a B now? Maybe a C?

How about joy? Are you easily irritated? If you're not sure, maybe ask your significant other. How much time do you spend complaining? How often do you laugh? Are you able to keep a positive attitude in times of frustration? Are you rationalizing your lack of joy right now?

Peace. How troubled or anxious are you? Are you concerned about the future of your local sports team? Concerned about the stock market or the price of gasoline? Fed up with politics and our current president?

Patience. Are you a peaceful, patient waiter? Have you already skipped ahead and finished your list? The other day I caught myself saying, "Come on; I don't have all day," to myself . . . about myself.

Kindness. How inclined are you to help someone even when you're busy or you know you won't get any credit? Do you notice people and listen to them? Are you thoughtful? Are you more likely to offer a criticism or a compliment?

Goodness. Are you giving of yourself, your time, your talents, your treasure? Is your heart getting larger or smaller, growing softer or harder, burning or turning cold?

Faithfulness. Are you dependable? Would other people say you are? Do you ever use your words to deceive others or put a spin on things that makes you look better than you actually are? Are you even doing this list with the rest of us?

Gentleness. Do you make sure your words are full of grace? Do you ever use words or actions that will inflict pain on someone else because it feels good to you? How often do you come alongside someone in pain and offer them comfort?

Self-control. Do you have any bad habits? Is lying one of them? Impulse-control issues? Do you ever fly off the handle and say or do something you later regret?

Last question: Do you feel inadequate at this point?

I do. I know me. I know what I'm like when I'm hungry or running late. I hear myself in traffic. I know what I say when you walk out of the room. Sometimes I start violating the fruit of the Spirit before I even get out of bed in the morning.

Now, at this point you might expect me to say some variation of this theme: Work harder. Suck it up, Buttercup, and try again—only this time pretend like you really mean it.

I'm not going to say that. I've heard it myself from too many people for too long, and I know from personal experience that it doesn't work. It's never worked—not for very long.

Instead, I'm going to point out something Jesus tells his friends in John 15. He says, "I am the vine, and you are the branches. Abide in me."

Question: What does a branch do?

Answer: it abides (or, as some versions render it, it remains). That is all.

I do not like this. Abiding seems so . . . passive . . . so . . . lazy. I want to look at whatever fruit I manage to bear and claim responsibility for it. See that fruit? I did that. It's because I worked so hard and did so much. That's why I have so much fruit. You're welcome.

Jesus says that's not how it works. The branch doesn't get credit because the branch doesn't produce jack. The vine gets all of the credit because the vine produces the fruit. The branch just stays attached to the vine. Fruit gets produced through the branch by the vine.

So, here's my job: stay connected. Keep receiving the flow of life and nourishment from God. If I will do that, I will grow. I won't be able to help it.

And I mean that in both senses—I won't be able to prevent it, and I won't be able to assist it. I just sit there, stay connected, abide.

The Dude abides, and so must I.

CHOOSING TO STAY CONNECTED

For those of you keeping score at home, I've just referenced Jesus, Yo-Yo Ma, Bobby McFerrin, Emeril Lagasse, and a Coen Brothers movie all in one chapter. Anyone have bingo?

If I fail to abide, I will stop growing. I will never change, and that's dangerous.

See, this is where the metaphor breaks down. A branch doesn't have much choice in the matter. I do. I can choose whether or not I stay connected. I can choose at any point in time to disconnect myself. I'm not talking about this in a salvific way; I'm talking about it in terms of my everyday life. I can choose today to wander off. I can choose to stray from the path. I can, and I have, told Jesus, "You stay here; I'm going over there for the weekend."

That conversation frequently serves as a preface to the stories behind the scars I have. "It all started when I told Jesus to hang tight while I detached myself from him and went inside this dark building for a couple of hours."

I have one job: stay connected to Jesus. Period. But I must warn you: even when I want to do this, it is much harder than it looks. Jesus is not easy to hold onto. Jesus goes into really bad neighborhoods after dark. He will put me in dangerous places. He rarely wants to stay inside my comfort zone. He likes to sleep in the arid places where the wild things are. He is unpredictable and elusive. I will have to pay very close attention to him in order to remain in him. I will get bumped and bruised. I may get beaten and left for dead. I may get killed. It's happened to people.

We don't talk about this enough in American Christianity, but we should. We prefer a Jesus who offers safety and comfort, a suburban, upper-middle-class Jesus who doesn't ask much more of us than that we be good citizens and decent neighbors. Go to church on Sunday. Maybe go on a mission trip to South America every once in a while.

People who chose to stay connected to Jesus have been beaten with sticks, flogged until they had no more skin left, set on fire, fed to wild animals, murdered in front of their children. And I'm not talking about stuff that happened two thousand years ago. Some of those things happened twenty minutes ago while you were reading this book. Some of it is happening right now.

Jesus does not offer us a problem-free existence on this planet. In fact, Jesus promises us the exact opposite. He says, "In this world, you will have trouble." That's the forecast: Trouble. Thanks, Jesus.

No one ever accused Jesus of being a Pollyanna optimist.

But he does say that if I want to bear fruit, if I want a life of real meaning and purpose, a life that cuts through all the bull and the smoke-and-mirrors, a life of gravitas and joy, the only way to get that kind of life is to stay connected to him, even when he veers off the beaten path onto the beating path.

Also, he offers me this, which might help: Jesus really wants to be with me. As hard as it may be to believe, he really likes me. He loves me. He wants to hang out with me. He tells his friends, "As the Father has loved me, so have I loved you" (John 15:9). This is staggering.

How much does the Father love Jesus? That's how much Jesus loves me. No matter where I've been or what I've done or how long it's been. As Michael Card puts it, Jesus proved that he would rather die than live without me. He loves me the way his Father loves him.

I'm a father. And I love my kids. In fact, sometimes I love them more when they've messed up! When kids are small, they love to show you some new skill they've learned. When they first learn to do a cartwheel, for example. "Daddy, watch this! Daddy, watch this!"

"Uh-huh, Sweetie. That's good," I say without even looking up from my laptop.

But let one of them get hurt in the backyard and scream, "Daddy, help!"

I will blow the door off its hinges to get to them if they're injured.

Think about that for a minute or two. When they want to show me something they're good at, I get bored pretty quickly. But when they are in trouble and need help . . . there is nothing in the world that will stand in my way.

This is how much God loves me.

I often try to pretend I am better than I am. I want to show God my cartwheels. And that doesn't get my Father's attention. But when I admit that I'm hurt and in trouble and I call out to him, there's nothing in the universe that will keep him from coming to help me.

This is why my prayers are precious to him—not because they're particularly eloquent. Rather, it is because he hears them through a Father's ears. The smallest detail of my life never gets old to God. The angels are probably sick of hearing about me. God can't help it; he's a Father.

NEVER ALONE

Do you know the most frequent promise in the Bible? It has nothing to do with the forgiveness of sins or the promise of eternal life. It is this: I will be with you.

Now, do you know the most frequent command in the Bible? Do not be afraid.

C'mon. There's got to be a connection there, right?

Why? Is everything going to turn out alright? Will I get through this safely? Will you not give me more than I can handle? Does everything happen for a reason that I'll understand in the great by-and-by? Can I just sit down and let you fight the battle for me? Will chariots of fire suddenly swoop in at the last minute and deliver me from the hands of my enemy? Can I count on you to protect my kids and my income and my two thousand four hundred-square-foot, four-bedroom, two-and-a-half-bath house?

No. None of that is promised to me. I may end up losing everything. And by "everything," I mean everything.

Every. Single. Thing.

My house, my job, my kids, my marriage, my reputation, my health, my car, my sense of identity, my security, my cognitive abilities. Everything.

But God does promise me this: God will be with me. No matter what happens. I need not fear because God is with me.

The psalmist said, "Even though I walk through the darkest valley, I will fear no evil" (Ps. 23:4). Why? Because I know "you are with me."

God was with Adam, Eve, Noah, Abraham, Joseph, Moses, David. Those folks lost an awful lot. They gained some things, too, but let's not sugarcoat this. There must have been times when Moses wondered if he would have been better off just ignoring that blasted burning bush in the desert. When Joseph got thrown in prison to rot, I bet he didn't console himself with the idea that at least God was still with him.

And then Jesus came and was given the name Immanuel—which means God is with us. And the people rejoiced. Until he died.

What must they have thought when a miracle-working man showed up and said, "I am God with you"? They must have been elated! He fed hungry people and healed sick people. He made blind people see. He gave hope to the hopeless. He took notice of the marginalized.

I bet they thought he was immortal. If he really was "God with us"—he had to be immortal, right? God cannot die. God certainly would never let human beings kill him.

And yet that is precisely what happened. No wonder they gave up and went back to fishing!

We forget that there wasn't a crowd of people waiting at the tomb on Sunday morning with a "WELCOME BACK, JESUS!!!" banner.

They thought he was "God with us" because he did amazing things, but when he died . . . they figured they must have been wrong about him. Jesus was a fake God. They had to think that. The only other option was that God did come among them and then died. Believing Jesus was a fake God was a better option than believing Jesus was a dead God.

A dead God won't do you any good. In fact, if God is dead, then there's no hope anymore. Evil has won; good has been defeated. If God is dead, then it's pretty much every man for himself from now on. Chaos. Disorder. Ruin. Meaninglessness. Survival of the fittest. That's the world if God is dead.

So, they figured they'd be better off choosing the other option. Jesus was a fake. Let's go back to fishing. Maybe the real God will actually show up some day and set us free. Until then, back to the nets, back to the salt mines, back to the humdrum routine of life.

But then Jesus showed back up. He suffered under Pontius Pilate, was crucified, dead and buried, he descended into hell and on the third day he rose again, demonstrating that not even death itself can keep God away from us. And almost immediately, he had to go looking for his friends who had scattered like a flock of sheep without a shepherd.

One of the things I love about the Bible is that it does not whitewash things to make the heroes more heroic than they really are. They mess up terribly. They have massive amounts of doubt—even after the resurrection. They get it wrong more often than they get it right. They break all the commandments, get themselves in over their heads, and then cry out to God who shows up in powerful and miraculous ways.

The Bible is not about people who want to be with God; it's about a God who wants to be with people and is willing to go to ridiculous lengths to do that. And I mean "ridiculous" in a literal sense. He subjected himself to ridicule on our behalf.

So, Jesus says, "Don't run off half-cocked and try to do this all by yourself. Abide with me. Talk. Pray. Listen. Eat. Stick with me. You do that, and growth not only will be normal, it will be unavoidable. You won't be able to help it. You'll just get big, big, big."

This is the tension we live in: we want to bear fruit, but we're told to abide.

TOO BUSY TO BE HAPPY

There have been seasons of my life when I have fallen for a lie. It was a simple lie, one that is propagated by our society, by our culture, by my religion sometimes. It seems like common sense, but it is, in fact, a dangerous and destructive lie. It goes like this: my happiness is dependent upon how busy I am.

Being busy means I'm important. Being busy means I'm using my time wisely. Busyness is worn like a badge of honor in our world. Any threat to that busyness is a threat to my hope for happiness.

There is one major problem with this thinking: being busy doesn't make me happy. It creates an illusion that I'm moving toward a day when I will feel happy—somewhere down the line—when I can finally slow down and be happy.

Busy today; happy tomorrow. But tomorrow never comes. Just more busyness. When I do coaching for leaders, one of the things I sometimes tell them is that they would be better leaders, they'd have better relationships, and they'd last longer in their field if they would simply slow down. But boy, oh boy, do people get defensive about their busyness. We have stuff to do, places to go, items to cross off our to-do lists, debt to eliminate, skills to master, promotions to earn, people to manage, dreams to chase. Go. Go. Go. Go. Go.

Think about the foolish idea of multitasking. Studies show that no one is good at it. And yet we persist, don't we? Even when it means never being present in an activity we enjoy. We feel guilty for having unplanned blocks of time. We scour the Internet looking for productivity hacks and apps. We check our email after hours, on weekends, even on vacation.

Part of this has to do with our idea of the American Dream—the notion that my potential for happiness is inextricably linked to my freedom to pursue health, wealth, and prosperity. I read something recently that said 80 percent of our nation believes they will one day become rich (the reality is that only about 10 percent will). It makes sense, then, for folks to live like they're in a race—constantly competing to beat the odds. I believe that if I work harder and longer than anyone else, squeeze more into my day than the guy in the cubicle next to mine, if I get up a little bit earlier and stay up a little bit later, then I'll be able to grab that brass ring and finally escape the busyness.

Life lived like that turns most of my days into something I must endure rather than something I could actually enjoy. Work is seen as a means to an end, rather than something that could be an end in and of itself. I think busyness leads to money, which will lead to happiness.

Someday.

I'm not saying there's no place for work. I want work that stretches me, work that fulfills me, work that infuses my life with meaning and purpose. But money won't ever lead me to happiness if I'm not happy already. And I won't be happy if I'm so busy that I can't pay attention to what's going on right now in this moment.

I think I'll be happier if I never have to work again, or if I didn't have bills, or if I had a bigger house or a boat or a houseboat. So, I spin my wheels trying to create a world that will allow me to kick back and breathe. Odds are, if I ever succeeded in creating such a place, I wouldn't know how to enjoy it. I've trained myself for barrenness through busyness.

It's time to take a long, hard look at what the American Dream means to me. I'm pretty sure there are parts of it that I'll have to work for. But I'm also pretty sure that there are parts of it that I already have if I'd slow down long enough to examine my life.

But who has time for that? We're all too busy being busy. It's like we're addicted to busyness. We believe that busyness will eventually lead to success, which will eventually lead to happiness. I've become convinced that the busier I am right now, the happier I will be—someday.

Busy today; happy tomorrow. But tomorrow never comes. Just more busyness.

Perhaps the worst thing imaginable would be to get to the end of my one and only life and realize I was so busy being busy that I never got around to being happy. I may have accomplished a great deal, but I never enjoyed it. I was never available to the people who matter most. I've never heard anyone on their deathbed say, "I wish I'd spent more time at the office."

Ironically, studies are beginning to show that busyness and success do not lead to happiness as much as happiness leads to greater effectiveness—in relationships and in our careers. As it turns out, it's more beneficial for us to shift our focus away from achieving happiness sometime in the future and toward figuring out how to access happiness in the here and now.

We've had it backward all along! Busy today; happy tomorrow—that doesn't work. Happy right now; successful tomorrow—that works much better nearly every time.

As I reflect on this, I realize that my life, when I'm only focused on getting things done, is not full of joy. I don't enjoy life; I put up with it. I see it as a necessary evil—something I have to do so I can get to something I want to do. I've spent most of my life doing the things I thought I had to do, and I have never gotten around to doing the things I enjoy.

Maybe later tonight. Or maybe over the weekend. Or maybe next summer during the once-a-year, over-scheduled, and under-funded family vacation.

When my days are consumed with things I have to do, I have little time for the things I want to do. I realize that discipline sometimes requires me to do things I must do in order to do the things I enjoy, but true happiness requires an understanding of the rhythm of life here. I need time with the people I love. I need space to do the things I enjoy. I sometimes need no agenda at all other than fun. I need the chance to explore and experience the world with curiosity and wonder.

Being able to do this, however, requires me to disconnect periodically from the world of busyness.

It's good to have dreams and goals. It's good to work toward those dreams and goals. Transformation does not come merely from the attainment of those dreams and goals but from the labor itself. Sometimes the effort is the reward.

But sometimes resting is the most transformative thing I can do.

"Abide in me," says Jesus, "and you will bear a lot of fruit. You won't be able to help it."

CHAPTER NINE

ADVENTURES IN MISSING THE POINT

Years ago, when my daughters were younger, my family's Saturday routine consisted of sleeping in a little, having a big breakfast together, and making assignments for what came to be known as "chore day." All the things that got piled up during the week would get unpiled on Saturday. Laundry would get done. Closets straightened out. Bathrooms scrubbed. You know the drill.

One Saturday, though, all this got interrupted before the first chore could begin. We were sitting at the breakfast table. I hadn't even managed to get my second cup of coffee before my next-door neighbor, Jim, rang the doorbell. In an incredibly calm and even voice he said, "John, I need you to run me to the hospital. I think I'm having a stroke."

He said it in the same way he might say, "John, I need you to run me to the grocery store. I think I need some milk."

I threw on a sweatshirt and a pair of jeans and spent the rest of the day in the Emergency Room. Oddly enough, forty-five minutes after we got there, he was fine. Something had certainly happened, but he was fine. Still, by then, he'd already had blood taken and was hooked up to the machine that goes "Ping!" So, we had to stay for a while. He tried to run me off, but I stubbornly refused. After all, if I went home, I'd have to scrub toilets.

I stayed, and we talked . . . about everything. Politics and religion (the two things you're not supposed to talk about in polite company). Jim was incredibly well-read and a deep thinker. He'd given up on church and was pretty sure Jesus was not God (a conviction solidified when his priest told him that no one in seminary believes that anymore, that seminary professors scoff at the idea, that the only reason anyone preaches it from the pulpit was because that's what they are paid to do).

Still, Jim was a believer of sorts. He knew there was a God. He believed that God had written something of a moral code on his heart. He actually said, "I've never doubted what the right thing to do is. I just can't seem to do what I know is the right thing." He didn't even know that his words came straight from the Bible (Romans 7 for those of you keeping score at home).

He was really concerned about the eternal destiny of his Muslim friend from work. He was still confused about why the Baptist church he grew up in fired the one pastor who connected with him. He didn't understand why religious people are so afraid of mystery. He was angry at television preachers who stole money from his aging relatives.

More than anything, he was worried that, after sixty-six years of pondering, he may not have made any progress at all in understanding this God who he is convinced exists. I suggested that maybe God really is infinite.

"I don't know, Jim. How do you measure progress against infinity?" I asked.

He laughed and said, "You may be my kind of preacher."

I took that as a compliment.

All of this brings up uncomfortable questions. Perhaps the most uncomfortable question of all is this: What's the point? What's the purpose of Christianity? What am I supposed to be doing? Why doesn't God just save us and then kill us? Why leave us here?

This book is based on the idea that at least part of the point is that I'm supposed to be becoming different, more like my Father in heaven, more like the great example and pattern that is Jesus.

But that's not what I see when I gaze out over the grand landscape that is Christendom. I'm not sure the reason millennials are fleeing our gatherings is because they encounter so many Jesus-like people there. In fact, it's probably more likely the opposite. They encounter petty, mean-spirited, morally judgmental, nitpicky people.

Nitpicky people are rarely invited to speak about big, global issues.

Sadly, it's not unusual for Christians to get all worked up over things that aren't really that big a deal. I remember the furor over *The Last Temptation of Christ*—which was actually a pretty decent book but a terrible movie. I remember thinking distinctly that if Christians hadn't made such a fuss, the movie would have just petered out on its own—and quickly. All that raising such a ruckus did was prolong the inevitable.

I honestly think people went to see that movie who wouldn't have if there hadn't been protests and picket lines at the movie theatre.

Did Christians learn their lesson? Nope. Anybody remember the hue and cry a few years ago over *The Da Vinci Code*? It was going to be the end of faith, leading our children astray. Churches would close. Western civilization would unravel. Christians would once again be thrown to the lions if this movie became a blockbuster hit.

I saw *The Da Vinci Code* the night it opened. I had a vested interest. I had been asked to write a book about the heretical worldview of Dan Brown, the author of the novel. I had written about and spoken about the movie for nearly two years before the movie came out, so I knew I had to see the film in order to respond to it with any kind of integrity.

So, I bought my ticket and lined up with lots of other folks. The theatre audience was at about 80 percent capacity. I was surprised to see how many people brought their kids with them. There was stuff in there that I didn't want my children to see, but . . . whatever.

To be honest, I didn't think the movie was very good. It was really long, and it felt like it ended three times. It just kept going and going and going. Ron Howard softened it a lot, and I think that made the story weaker than it should have been. But that's just my opinion.

It wasn't terrible, but it wasn't very good, either.

That weekend I had a conversation with some folks who actually went out and protested. They made signs about how *The Da Vinci Code* crucified Christ all over again. They handed out tracts to anyone who came close and shouted at people who stayed far away. I don't think they deterred anyone from seeing the movie—it made more than $77 million in its opening weekend.

And it got me scratching my head over what a "Christian response" to something like that movie ought to look like. Most of the people I spoke with suggested what amounts to a "religious" response. But few of those people suggested anything distinctively Christian.

See, a Christian is someone who has made a commitment to follow Jesus, to imitate him in his thoughts and values and actions. So, when we ask what a Christian response to *The Da*

Vinci Code should look like, we're really asking WWJDWTDVC: What Would Jesus Do With The Da Vinci Code?

Maybe it's just me, but I have a hard time imagining Jesus picketing or being so casual with the language of crucifixion. I have a hard time imagining him handing out tracts or shouting at people from a distance. Those tactics seem too mean-spirited and impersonal for what I know of Jesus's character and personality.

Sure, Jesus turned over tables and chased people with a whip once, but he is also the same guy who, while hanging on the cross, looked out at the very people who had just finished flogging him and were now killing him by the most excruciating means imaginable and asked that they be forgiven, because, after all, they didn't realize what they were doing.

THE GOAL OF CHRISTIANITY

Let's back up a little and talk about what it means to read or watch or listen or converse Christianly. What I mean is that Christians (in my opinion) ought to have a different perspective from the rest of the world when we are reading or watching or listening or conversing. We could start by answering this question: What is the goal of life for a Christian?

My friend Ken Boa says that the goal of the Christian life is to become progressively conformed to the image of Christ. To do this, we must learn to love God completely, others compassionately, and ourselves correctly. Doing this brings glory to God.

Various writers, speakers, and churches have expressed this in different words. They've talked about the inward, outward, and upward focus of Christianity. They've talked about growing in intimacy with God, community with other Christians, and influence with those outside of the Christian faith. They've used five Gs or five Ms or different shapes and colors. It all comes down to the same thing: Love God and Love People.

So, if the goal for Christians is to learn how to better appreciate, appropriate, and reciprocate love—to be better lovers of God and others—then why do we read anything at all? Why do we read the Bible? Why do we read devotional materials? Why do we listen to sermons, watch television shows and movies, or have conversations with others?

Why not take a vow of silence and move to a cave in the wilderness until Jesus returns? Mmmmmm . . . let me just sit here for a second with that thought because right now it sounds kind of good. Cave. Wilderness. Silence. Deep breath.

. . .

. . .

. . .

. . .

Okay, where was I?

Ah, yes . . .

My theory is that we do these things, to various degrees, not just because we've become like Jesus and are behaving like he did, but we do these things *in order to* become like him.

Not merely to learn more about him—though that is important, too. Certainly not to check the boxes and make ourselves look spiritual. We read our Bibles and devotional materials, we listen to sermons and Christian music in order to become more like Jesus. In other words, all these things are a means to an end. The end is our transformation into Christlikeness.

At least, that's how it's supposed to work.

But it's not just Christian materials or things found in your local Christian bookstore that help make you more like Jesus. In fact, I could say that some of what you'll find there might actually be counterproductive if you're not careful. I've certainly found this to be the case. That's why I'm stuck in the mess I'm in. I did read the Bible front to back. I read it chronologically. I read it in the original languages. I've logged more hours in Christian bookstores than I am comfortable admitting. I've spent tens of thousands of dollars supporting the Christian subculture of books, music, movies, and art.

Maybe I should put quotation marks around "art"—there wasn't always a lot of art to it. It was often not much more than a visual sermon with very little care given to aesthetics. And I still have no idea where the line between "music" and "Christian music" lies. A lot of it started to sound like "Jesus is my girlfriend" songs—where you just take a standard love song and substitute Jesus for the name of your object of affection.

I even have some Christian jazz somewhere. Again, how those songs are Christian, I will never know. Melody, rhythm, harmony, chord structures, syncopation—it's hard to make a case that these things are "Christian" in any real sense of the word. Perhaps it's just jazz music by jazz musicians who happen to be Christian. But I digress.

It is also possible for you to read the newspaper, watch CNN, binge watch a show on Netflix, and listen to talk radio in a way that helps you become more like Jesus.

Certainly, there are times when I just want to check out, put my brain in park, and watch Bugs Bunny thwart the best efforts of Elmer Fudd. Sometimes mindless spectacle is just what the doctor ordered. But there are important books to be read and inspiring movies to watch—some explicitly Christian, others not. There are funny jokes to be told, but there are also important conversations to be had.

But there is a way to read, a way to watch, and a way to listen that must be unique to those who have signed up to follow and become transformed from within into the likeness of Jesus.

READING THE BIBLE CHRISTIANLY

Once, a church I served gave away three hundred Bibles. People signed up to read three chapters a day to get through the whole Bible in a year. They even created a blog to help folks. As far as I know, it lasted all of three months.

Don't get me wrong: I think it's a good idea to read the Bible on a regular basis. But it can be a hindrance to my spiritual formation if I read the Bible the wrong way. Honestly, some of the meanest people I've ever met know a lot of Bible verses and have read the Good Book cover to cover. Certainly, the Pharisees in Jesus's day were familiar with the Scriptures, but they had little love for God and even less love for people. They engaged in spiritual disciplines like prayer, tithing, and fasting, but they didn't do them to bring glory to God. They were interested in bringing glory to themselves.

Obviously, there is a way to read or give or pray that brings glory to God, and there is a way that does not.

As I read my Bible, I must keep the goal in mind. The goal is never to simply get through the daily allotted portion and check the box; the goal has to be bigger and deeper than that. Remember, we've said that the goal of life for Christians is to bring glory to God by becoming progressively more and more like him—to become godlier people. The most substantial and practical byproduct of that godliness is that I'll find myself growing in my ability to love and be loved by God and others.

That's the goal of life for Christians, and that should be the goal for my Bible reading as well. And my movie watching. And my conversations.

If godliness or Christlikeness is the goal, then I'll read the Bible in a particular way. I'll read it with my eyes open, scouting for clues as to what he is like. I'll conclude my reading by asking myself, "What does this portion teach me about the character and nature of God?" Then, as I attempt to apply the passage to my life, I'll ask, "How does this portion help me grow in my ability to love and be loved by God and others?"

This approach to a daily Bible reading differs tremendously from approaches I've tried before. And I wonder what might happen if a whole church chose to read through the Bible together for a year with this lens in place. Now, what if I did more than just read the Bible this way? What if I read other materials this way? What if you read this book that way? What if I read Max Lucado or John Piper or Rob Bell that way?

What if my first question had nothing to do with whether I think the author is right or wrong or agrees with me or not? What if it had everything to do with finding an aspect of God's character to become enthralled with, and with learning to love and be loved by God and others to a greater degree—even when that lesson comes from an author I don't much care for?

I'm not saying we have to mindlessly accept and agree with everything we read, and God knows we need discernment. There's a time to take a stand for orthodoxy, and there's a time to confront heresy. But I'm concerned that all too often I approach reading material looking for error. I practice what we could call a hermeneutic of suspicion. As if I'm God's appointed theological spell-check program, I read things to either confirm what I already believe or to gain ammunition in some sort of war of words.

I know I've been guilty of that. But can that be considered "reading Christianly"? That answer is pretty obviously "no."

Being a Christian comes down to glorifying God by becoming progressively more and more like him—particularly in my ability to love and be loved by God and others. If that's so, then just about anything I read should be read with that end in mind—whether it is the Bible or any kind of spiritually-formative material. I should always read with my eyes open to learn more about God's character and nature, and I should always ask myself how the material I've just read can assist me in my efforts to grow in love. I would hasten to add that this applies to me as I listen to a sermon.

LISTENING TO SERMONS CHRISTIANLY

As a guy who speaks in just about every kind of church you can imagine, I cannot tell you how many people seem to listen at me rather than listening to (or even with) me. They sit there, arms folded, listening for error or listening to make sure I touch all the appropriate bases. They listen to sermons the way an umpire watches a baseball game. They don't listen for personal transformation. They don't listen to grow.

These are the people who always want clarification on some fine point of something I said in passing that wasn't even the point I was trying to make. These are the people who want to know what version of the Bible I was reading from and why. These are the people who want to know where I went to seminary. These are also the people who wish their brother-in-law had heard the message. They want to get a copy of the CD for someone at work, because it was just the sort of message someone else needed to hear.

These people never come and tell me that it was just what they needed to hear. They never tell me how they could grow from the message or how they plan on applying it to their lives.

Please understand that not everyone does this. There are also plenty of folks who listen well and humbly seek to apply whatever truth they find in the sermons they hear to their personal lives. I love these people, and I wish I were more like them.

I am as guilty of this error as anyone else. One of the things I do—as part of my work—is critique sermons. Preachers often pay me to give them advice or help or coaching in becoming better communicators. Sadly, it has become difficult for me to listen to a sermon for spiritual formation now, because I'm always thinking about how the speaker could have communicated his/her points more effectively.

But what would change if I started listening to sermons the way I just suggested we ought to read? What if I first asked myself, "What does this sermon teach me about the character and nature of God?" And second, "How can I apply this sermon in such a way as to help me grow in my ability to love and be loved by God and others?"

Maybe this would eliminate a lot of the bickering and divisiveness Christianity currently experiences. Here, at last, is a way for Calvinists and Arminians to read one another without feeling the need to get all bent out of shape. The Piper-ites and the Bell-eons can listen to and with one another, rather than simply listening at one another.

If they choose to. Sadly, I doubt they will. But love believes all things, so I will continue to hope toward that end.

THE MOST CONVINCING THOUGHT

Don't rush past that thought too quickly. The Bible says, "[Love] believes all things" (1 Cor. 13:7 NASB).

But I don't.

Obviously, the Bible's not talking about being naïve. I think the Bible is saying that love always believes the best; love gives the beloved the benefit of the doubt.

But I don't.

Well, I do. I usually give my kids the benefit of the doubt when they're talking to me. I give my girlfriend the benefit of the doubt when I read an email from her. When my best friend sends me a confusing text message, I give him the benefit of the doubt. I do this with people I love. I just don't love many people.

What if I chose to love more people? What if I chose to love authors and speakers and filmmakers and song writers in this way? What if reading and listening became for me an act of Christian love?

That's the most convicting thought I've had this year. I remember where I was sitting when it hit me. And since then, I've been trying to make some changes.

Now, as I read an author or listen to a speaker or have a conversation, I'm trying to get myself out of a judgmental posture and ask myself, "How would I read this if I loved the author? How would I listen if I loved this speaker?"

I am an author and a professional speaker—that's what I'll put on my tax form this year. And I have to say: getting up to speak in front of a group of people is one of the most nerve-wracking endeavors imaginable. A close second would be actually sitting down and putting thoughts on paper for people to read. I am vulnerable when I do that. I am especially vulnerable to criticism immediately after I'm done. And, having worked with pastors and preachers from Seattle to Orlando, I know that I am far from alone.

There are books I disagree with. There are speakers who spout error of all kinds. There is a time for healthy disagreement and even for confrontation and rebuttal. But I have been humbled and convicted by God about the way I read and the way I listen. All too often, I listen for a chance to disagree, confront, and rebut. I sit, like Simon Cowell, listening for a mistake, hoping they're off-key so I can appear witty, intelligent, and superior.

I'm not rooting for the speaker. I'm not loving the author. And that—most assuredly—is not living Christianly.

The Bible says flatly, "The only thing that counts is faith expressing itself through love" (Gal. 5:6). That's what comes when I am fully submerged in the grace of God, in the unmerited, unearned favor of my Creator and Redeemer. When you finally get grace—or when grace finally gets you—you find it impossible to sit in judgment of someone else. You realize that you're not "in" because you're smarter than someone else or more theologically precise in your terminology.

Sitting in judgment like that becomes repulsive to you because you realize it's usurping the role of the One who has the right to sit in judgment of you but has extended mercy and kindness, forgiveness and love instead.

Jesus seemed to think that acceptance and forgiveness could accomplish what judgment and condemnation never could. When I become like him, I'll begin to see things that way, too.

CHAPTER TEN

LOVING ME

So, I had this conversation with myself recently. Don't act like I'm the only one who does this. You talk to yourself, and you probably answer back. Don't even try to deny it.

The conversation with myself went like this:

ME: What are you doing?
ME: I'm looking for love.
ME: How's that going?
ME: Not well.
ME: How long have you been at it?
ME: About forty-seven years now.
ME: Have you found it yet?
ME: I found it for a little while. It was amazing, but it didn't last. I screwed it up.
ME: Why don't you stop?
ME: Because I really want to find it again. It was the best thing ever.

ME: What if looking for love is the kind of thing that's keeping you from finding it?

ME: Well . . . that would be a big bucket of yuck.

The more I thought about it, the more I began to wonder if maybe I was onto something. Could it be that looking for love, like working for transformation, is the very thing that prevents me from finding love? Could it be that looking for love isn't how you find love?

I now know I've been believing this lie that love is "out there"—which means, of course, that love is not "in here." So, I've been looking for love without realizing that love is here beside me, above me, beneath me, within me. To quote one of my favorite bands from high school (Everything but the Girl): "Love is here where I live."

But I don't always trust this. Truth be told, I don't always trust it because I don't always feel lovable. So much junk and baggage from my past conspires against me to keep me believing that love is not here with me—that love is somewhere out there—and that I will only find love after I prove myself through some long and arduous ordeal.

But I've done that. I've tested my mettle. I've sailed the seven seas, jousted with windmills, tamed a dragon or two, spoken in tongues, walked through fire, and still . . . nothing.

Actually . . . not nothing.

What I've learned is that I'm a little like Dorothy in Oz. I had the power all along. I didn't need to go on some terrible quest.

Not too long ago, I texted Tiffany and said, "I think I get it. I'm enough already. I don't have to try to be more than I am. In fact, it's when I'm trying to be more than I am that I always end up shooting myself in the foot."

She wrote back, "You sure are a slow learner." Actually, in her inimitable way, she used a colorful adjective, which my editor has chosen to expunge from the record.

Regardless, sometimes I am, my dear. Sometimes I am.

LOVE NOTES FROM ALONG THE WAY

Here are a few notes from my journal for you to consider—things I've learned about love.

1. Looking for love is like voluntarily going to hell. The search for love comes from forgetting who you are, where you've come from, where you're going, and what love actually is. You go looking for love when you've fallen from grace and are afraid that love has abandoned you. Or you go looking for love because you know what it feels like to have someone look at you and say, "Take him away. Give him to someone else. I don't want him."

That's the struggle adopted kids like me don't often talk about. I know it probably didn't play out like that, but in my head and in my heart, it might as well have. For whatever reason, you believe that you exist outside of love. I am "here"—love is "there"—and I can't seem to figure out how to get inside.

I'm like an orphan kid with his nose pressed to the window. You become consumed with trying to get inside that house, and—if you could ever con or sneak or trick someone into letting you in—you must do everything in your power to stay there. Do not make yourself too much of a nuisance. Make sure you are pulling your own weight. Make sure you are earning your keep. If you become too much of a bother, they might decide to put you on someone else's doorstep.

It happened before.

2. Looking for love is terrifying. I am convinced that the most fundamental and existential fear a human can experience is the notion that I am unlovable, that some defect deep down in me makes people look at me and withhold love from me. This one fear gives rise to all the other fears and anxieties I've dealt with for nearly fifty years. Fear of abandonment. Fear of not mattering or measuring up. Fear of discovery. Fear of intimacy. Fear of authenticity. It all comes from this underlying sense that I am—at my core—unlovable.

Of course, this fear is a ghost—or, rather, it is what people considered a ghost but was more likely just a sheet flapping in the wind. If you could find the courage to approach it and embrace it, you'd learn that it has no power. But you'll never know that if you're afraid to examine it closely.

So, you leave it alone and pretend it doesn't exist. And you go looking for someone you might be able to convince that you are, in fact, lovable. Do whatever you must. Say whatever you must. Trick them if you have to. Earn it. And then make sure they never find out that you fooled them into loving you. If they ever figure it out, they'll leave you for sure.

3. Ultimately, looking for love hurts. Until you change your mind about your own fundamental level of lovability, you'll always need someone else to overturn that self-pronounced judgment. You'll create a fake self. You'll hide your pain and your dark matter. You'll seduce. You'll draw attention. You'll win admiration. But because it's not the real you, it won't ever attract real love. And you'll always have this suspicion that if the other person knew the truth about the real you, they'd leave you just like everyone else has.

So, even when you're with this person, you'll keep your eyes peeled for where you'll go next once this one dumps you. You'll always be waiting for the other shoe to drop. You'll flinch all the time. You'll be super-defensive.

And because you never change your mind about yourself, all you find is more evidence of your own unlovableness.

4. It's so hard to believe in true love while you're looking for it. The more you look, the less you experience it. And the less you believe you're worthy of it. You begin to doubt it's even possible for someone to love you. If they say they do, they probably have some agenda. You may even begin to wonder if love exists.

That is the worst pain of all. You cannot live like that. You may continue to breathe and have a heartbeat, but you wither from the inside out. You end up a shell, a shadow of yourself.

I know. I've been there and done that.

You don't get out of hell by your own effort; you get out of hell by surrendering. You don't find love by looking for it; you find true love by discovering the things you're doing that keep you from experiencing the love you already have—the things that keep you from being who you already are. You begin to find love when you remember that you come from love, you're headed to love, you are made with love, for love, by love. In a sense, you are love.

Think how different life would be if you stopped trying to be loving toward other people (and yourself) and simply tried to be love in their presence. Stop. Think about that. This is a huge paradigm shift. Don't rush through it.

This all begins with casting off the lie that you are unworthy of love, unable to love, unlovable. Ultimately, the goal is not to find love; it is to know love. This starts when you stop looking for love.

SEEING PURELY: LOVE WITHOUT A MASK

The first time I ever met my oldest daughter is among the most memorable moments in my life. She was the first blood relative

I'd ever known, and I held her there in the hospital for what felt like an eternity—her eyes darting in every direction until they locked on mine. I know she couldn't focus on me, but it seemed like she was peering right through me. It was magical.

Babies are amazing. We watch their every moment with joy. We study them while they sleep. We celebrate every new thing as if it were the most momentous occasion.

And yet . . .

Can we be honest about something? Objectively speaking, babies are not much to look at. They're short and chubby and toothless. They don't have much hair, and they leak out of both ends. When you really look at a baby, she almost appears to be slightly out of focus. And babies clearly have no idea what to do with their bodies.

Still, they are so fully alive—so filled with life—they almost seem to vibrate. They contain within them, to use the words of Thomas à Kempis, a lively flame that is never wearied or confounded.

Also, nothing is ever as naked as a baby. When a baby is naked, it's not just the absence of clothing that you notice—it's the absence of self-consciousness. A baby is not just nude; a baby has no mask, no pretense, no armor. Buddhists would say that a baby is still wearing the Original Face. Babies know nothing of facial management. You've never seen a baby with a good poker face. It's all right there for you to see.

Furthermore, babies do not care if you know everything about them. Babies aren't the least bit interested in trying to be someone they are not. They don't know how to look good or to be more interesting than they are. They have no pretense, no deception, no attempt to create a more appealing persona. Babies don't know if they are black or white, Asian or Latino. Babies don't even know if they're Christian or Muslim. They haven't had time to hear a story about how depraved they are or how unworthy. They haven't been told yet that love is fleeting and elusive. Babies don't judge you. They're not cynical. They harbor no grudges.

A baby does not try to be lovable; a baby simply is.

And this is what draws us to them, like moths to a flame. When you look at a baby, you see what Francis of Assisi referred to as humanity's eternal loveliness. You see it because—unless you're a doctor—you are not really looking at a baby with your eyes but with your heart.

And what is it we hope to see?

I think I hope to see a little bit of my own eternal loveliness. I think I want to be reminded that the same things that are in a baby—the very things that make babies so attractive to us—are also in me. Always have been. Always will be.

My theology tells me that God (who is Love) extended himself in love in the act of creation, which means that everything he created was created by Love, with Love, for Love. There are no exceptions to this. You come from love. You are headed to love. You're meant for love in the meantime. That's origin, destiny, and morality: love, love, and love.

Everybody's basic truth is: I am lovable. This is true whether you believe it or not, whether you know it or not, whether you remember it or not. Sadly, my daughter—like all babies—grew up and was told a lot of untruths about love. It's possible to believe a lot of wrong things about oneself and about one's lovability. It's possible to believe that love is hard and brittle and full of thistles and must be earned by the sweat of one's brow. It's possible to begin to doubt the existence of love, or—worse—to believe that love is only meant for others. It's possible for a baby to grow up and believe the lie that says, "You are unlovable." Perhaps this is what Jesus had in mind when he told us to become like little children. Children don't ever think they have to earn love. It would never occur to them on their own to believe that love would ever be withheld from them.

Like a baby, I was made by Love. I am made of Love. I am made to Love.

When I remember that, I can realize that I already know how to love and be loved in return. Only then can I follow Bob Goff's advice to "give away love like you're made of it" (@bobgoff, May 29, 2015).

MY LITTLE SECRET

When I was younger, I had a problem, and I knew it. I didn't know what the problem was exactly, but I knew I had a problem. I was anxious. I was insecure. At times, I felt invisible. Other times I felt like I was in a fishbowl. Preachers' kids often experience this. I know there were a lot of times when I tried too hard to be liked. I know there were other times when I went out of my way to let others know I didn't really care what they thought of me (even though I secretly did).

There was a moment that happened when I was in high school. My family had moved from Southern California to Gwinnett County, Georgia—talk about culture shock! I could not seem to fit in, and I desperately wanted to. I finally had an adult tell me something that really hurt. It was necessary, but it hurt. I was asking this guy why I couldn't seem to make friends, why I couldn't fit in, why I never got the girl, why other guys who weren't as smart or as athletic or as witty always got what I wanted.

He thought for a moment, and then he asked me, "Do you really want to know?"

"Yes!" I blurted out.

He took a deep breath, looked me in the eye, and said, "It's because you don't love yourself."

It was like someone had punched me in the gut. He wasn't being unkind; he was making an honest observation. And he was right. I could never have said, "I love myself," and felt okay saying it. In fact, I had lived for a long time with the understanding that loving yourself was a bad thing. One of the worst things you could say to someone was, "You must really love yourself." Loving yourself was morally wrong, conceited, sinful, blasphemous.

Or so I thought.

I did not love myself. That was my dirty, little secret. I tried to cover it up by being popular, by being good at sports, by singing in a band, by managing others' perceptions of me. I worked hard to be a good son, a good student, and a good friend. But mostly, I did what I thought people wanted me to do—so that they would love me. I was terrified of disapproval and rejection, and I did everything I could do to avoid them.

I wasn't a bad person. I hadn't really done anything wrong. I had no idea why I felt this way. I just did. I felt that love had to be earned, and it had to come from somewhere "out there." If someone had asked me to name something I loved about myself, I wouldn't have had an answer. Honestly, I didn't know who I was. I was too busy trying on different personas that I thought were more lovable than my true identity.

I did not love myself. You cannot love someone you don't know.

This conversation—this revelation—sent me on a journey. I began to read things about love. I read Leo Buscaglia. I read Lao Tzu. I read Viktor Frankl and Elie Wiesel and Erich Fromm. I read Søren Kierkegaard and C. S. Lewis and Henri Nouwen and Brennan Manning and Lewis Smedes. And something started to happen inside of me. I started to unlearn some things, and I started to relearn some things. And I started to understand what it might mean to love myself.

And then something else happened: my education introduced me to a brand of contemporary American evangelical theology which was heavily influenced by Reformed thinking and neo-Fundamentalism. I began to read and write about my depravity and how unworthy and unlovable I am by nature. I began to believe again that I did not deserve love, that I was lucky to be alive, that I should be grateful for whatever crumbs fell my way. Just like that, all the anxiety of my youth came flooding back—only this time it was more theologically informed.

I came to feel as though self-love could be possible only as a consequence—it was an effect, not a cause. I could love myself if someone I respected loved me first. I could love myself if my parents loved me, if my wife loved me, if my professors loved me, if my congregation loved me, if my publisher loved me. How I felt about me was determined by how someone else felt about me and how I felt about them.

I was back to being terrified of disapproval and rejection, back to managing others' perceptions of me, back to doing what I thought people wanted me to do—so that they would love me. It was awful. It was scary. It was exhausting. It was also completely unnecessary.

Thankfully, I now have a strong therapist named Bill who is fluent in theology and can remind me of the good, the true, and the beautiful. Tiffany tells me that if I ever begin to doubt the existence of God, all I have to do is remember that I picked my therapist out of the back of a copy of *Psychology Today*.

I've been on a journey unlearning and relearning so much about love, and I've had a lot of help. Mostly what I'm rediscovering is that love is not "out there"—it's right here. I'm also learning that nearly every significant problem I've ever experienced in my life comes from a lack of love. I help people with addiction, unemployment, divorce, debt, loneliness—those are the presenting problems. Underneath those problems, there's a lack of wholeness, a fear of being unlovable, and the desire for happiness, meaning, and purpose.

When I talk to people about love, it makes them feel better about themselves, and it helps them deal with their problems more effectively. Karl Menninger said, "Love cures people, both the ones who give it and the ones who receive it." Love heals. Love restores. I believe love is the solution to all of our problems.

WHAT ABOUT YOU?

I am now in a position to say that the quality of your relationship with yourself determines the quality of your relationship with everyone (and everything) else. Your love of yourself (or lack thereof) determines your physical health, your diet, your exercise, and your financial well-being. This influences the pace of your life, your relationship with God, your creativity, your happiness.

Jesus instructs us to love our neighbors as we love ourselves. If some of us tried to do that, our neighbors might very well say, "No, thank you." Perhaps this is why we have so little influence in our communities; we are loving our neighbors the way we love ourselves—by neglecting them and uttering abusive language toward them.

When you know that love doesn't come to you from "out there," you don't have to stalk people, put them on a pedestal, or idolize them. Nor do you have to belittle or put them down to make yourself feel better. You can treat people as equals. You don't have to put on a show or do certain things to gain their approval. You can love with no strings attached. You can make different choices about who you give your phone number to, who you text, who you date, who you have sex with and when, who your friends are, and when it's right to stay in a relationship—or leave one.

When you love yourself, you stop playing a role in order to be more deserving of love from others. You can receive love. You won't be threatened by too much love. You can recognize when you're being loved—and when you're being used.

When you remember that you have come from love, you are headed to love, and you are where you are for love . . . then you can begin to love who you are and where you are.

I used to meditate a lot. I probably should try to pretend that I still do, but the truth is I don't. I became an intellectual a few years back, and most intellectuals don't meditate. Intellectuals read and study and ponder. Meditation is for people who are "spiritual but not religious"—and I have qualms with that phrase. I think a lot of people hide behind it.

I did.

But, as I said, I'm on a journey of sorts now—an odyssey. That's what Bill calls it. And I find that my journey is somehow taking me both forward and backward simultaneously. I'm moving forward in ways I could not have imagined, but, as I do so, I find myself drawn back in time to things I cherished, things I practiced, things I desired and pursued as a younger version of myself. Some of those things are childish and should be put away. Some of those things, however, are childlike and should be recaptured.

I used to meditate a lot, and I think meditation is one of those things that I need to recapture in order to be the real me that I once was and that I sometimes still am but that I would like to be more often. Meditation, for me, reminds me of things—deep things—things that are vitally important for me.

I remember asking a teacher once about meditation. I had thought that the point was to clear one's mind of all thought. As an anxious person with a busy mind, I find this impossible to do. My teacher gave me this suggestion: rather than trying to stop your thoughts when you meditate, focus your attention on the most important thing in life.

For me, that means love. Meditation isn't me trying to enter into a clear, blank space; meditation is a chance for me to focus all my thoughts on love. What is love? What does love feel like, smell like, sound like? What does love do?

My theology tells me that God is love. Everything God does, he does from love and with love. Everything God touches has the fingerprints of love—a residue of love—on it and in it. This includes me. This includes you. This includes my friend. This includes my enemy. As I begin to think with God, then, I begin to see the love of God everywhere I look.

Even when I look at myself.

Perhaps this is what Paul meant when he said that it's possible to take on the mind of Christ—a mind that sees things through the lens of love in all situations and circumstances. I find that when I am able to tune into love in this way, I let go of cynicism, judgment, self-criticism, feelings of unworthiness, resentment, fear.

THE PRESENT LOVE OF GOD

On my way to becoming a bona fide intellectual, I continue to read a lot of books. As I've mentioned before, I read for the sole purpose of critiquing a book—usually from a "Christian perspective" (as if there is only one perspective that would qualify as Christian). I remember when a concerned mother showed up in my office begging me to read this novel about a young boy studying to become a wizard. Surely this book would encourage children to explore the dark arts of Wiccan Magick! That was the most preposterous thing I had ever heard, but I dutifully read the novel and gave my report, suggesting that Harry Potter had more in common with the literature of C. S. Lewis than with the literature of Anton LaVey.

That did not go over well.

One book I read during that time period was called *A Course in Miracles*. It has been built up and torn down plenty of times by plenty of people. And I find it to be vague and New Agey. But I also find a lot of Jesus in it. Go ahead. Report me to the Evangelical neo-Fundamentalist authorities. There's Jesus in that book. There's other stuff, too, but there's no denying there is Jesus in there.

For example, the book says, "You are the work of God, and His work is wholly lovable and wholly loving. This is how a man must think of himself in his heart, because this is what he is."

That sounds downright Jesusy to me.

The book also says that you have two selves: one is real; the other is imaginary. The real self is the you God made you to be. The imaginary self is your ego. The real you is made of love. The fake you is made of fear. To quote the book: "You have but two emotions [love and fear]. One you made and one was given you. Each is a way of seeing, and different worlds arise from their different sights."

That's profound right there. That's . . . dare I say . . . biblical.

The book goes on to say:

> Put all your faith in the love of God within you; eternal, changeless and forever unfailing. This is the answer to what confronts you today. Through the Love of God within you, you can resolve all seeming difficulties without effort and in sure confidence. Tell yourself

> this often today. It is a declaration of release from the belief in idols. It is your acknowledgment of the truth about yourself.

That sounds like a mashup of Philippians and 1 John.

Sometimes when I'm in church, I'll hear someone invite God to be present. I know what they mean, but this is just theologically wrong. God is present. In fact, to use theologically precise language, we say that God is omnipresent—he's always and everywhere. You don't invite God's presence; you recognize God's presence, like Jacob at Bethel.

Since God is love, this means that love is also present—right here—right now—in me—around me. Love is here where I live, so I don't have to invite it or summon it from "out there"—I simply need to recognize it "in here." Love is not a technique you learn or a secret you discover after a long and arduous journey. Love is present, and love will teach you how to love.

Moreover, if you really want to know what love is, you must be willing to live your love. If I am going to grow in love—in my ability to love and be loved in return (which seems to me to be the point of Christianity), I must set my mind on this one intention: find someone to love in word and deed. Be love incarnate for someone. Embody love for that person. Love is more than an intellectual exercise. It does no good to love everyone in general if you never get around to loving someone specifically.

Find someone. Determine to love them. Live your love.

LOVING YOUR WORLD

One last thing: in order to love myself, I have to love where I am.

As I've mentioned before, when I was young, my family lived in West Monroe, Louisiana. This is not a bad place, but we did not like it. In fact, we called it "Lousy-ana" when I was a kid.

Please, save me the hate mail. I love going back to visit, and I see that part of the world with vastly different eyes now. I am merely telling you how it was.

I've since had the chance to live in a lot of other places. Southern California. East Texas. Columbia, Maryland. Atlanta, Georgia. My family moved to the Atlanta area from California when I was in high school. It was a rough transition for me, and I could not wait to get back to the West Coast. I graduated from high school and packed up my Hyundai and headed for Pepperdine University.

After school, I got married and moved back to Atlanta when my wife got a job here. We left, and then we came back. This became a pattern for me. I would leave Atlanta only to return a few years later. In 2012, I moved back, and I think I might be here to stay now. In fact, when I returned, I went to see my friend and chiropractor Lee Strickland. When he saw me, he said, "Dude, you've been trying to leave Atlanta since I met you in 1986. When are you gonna get it through your head that this is where you're supposed to be?"

I feel like I spent a lot of my life running from where I was—being discontent—my eyes scanning the horizon for the next thing, the next person, the next job, the next opportunity. I never spent much time being where I was. I certainly didn't spend much time loving where I was. And that led to a feeling of rootlessness.

I get to travel a lot nowadays. Speaking engagements and consulting allow me to see the whole wide world, and I notice this same tendency in a lot of people. Some people truly hate where they are. I'll ask them, "So, what's there to do in this town? What makes this place special?" They'll look at me in response and say, "Nothing! No one ever comes here. No one even likes it here."

I can't help but wonder why these people stay. It's not like their wagon broke down here. People are mobile. You can move. But some people would rather stay somewhere they're miserable than take a risk and go somewhere better—or at least better for them.

That's a big thing to remember: there's no better or worse really when it comes to where you are. There's better for you. There's worse for you. What's better for you might be worse for someone else—and vice versa. Also, what's better for you now may be worse for you later. Things happen. People show up. You land in places for a reason and for a season. Sometimes that season is life-long; oftentimes it is not. But it is possible to love where you are. And there are three ways you can show love for where you are right now—even if you think it's not ideal.

1. You can love where you are by owning it. Own where you are. You didn't land there by chance or accident. You are where you are because of the choices you have made. You have allowed yourself to end up where you are right now. Own it. That house. That car. That couch. Those curtains. That spouse. Those children. This job. The food in your pantry. The money in your bank account. The debt. The clothes. Your current weight. Your hairstyle. The restaurants nearby. The museums or the wide-open spaces or the 360-degree horizon or the skyscrapers—all of that stuff that makes up where you are—own it. That's the first step to loving where you are. Own it.

2. You can love where you are by fixing it. If you don't like the stuff where you are, make something better. If there's no museum, build one. If there's no green space, make one. If you don't like your relationship, change it (and really, I mean change your part of it—you can't fix someone else, and if you try, you'll just mess it up even worse). If you want a better job, create one for yourself.

You have far more control over your life than you believe. You can decide today that your life is not going to continue the way it has. You can change. You don't have to be stuck. Go to the gym. Start saving money. Pay off your debt. Buy some fresh flowers. Paint the room. Stop blaming others for where you are, and start changing things for the better. That's the second stop to love where you are: fix it.

3. You can love where you are by leaving it. I know that sounds odd, but sometimes the most loving thing you can do is leave. Sometimes people don't cooperate with change. Sometimes people don't want to get better. Sometimes your job or your location likes itself exactly the way it is, and if you try to evolve, it will kill you.

Leave. Your wagon isn't broken down. You can go, but, if you do, make sure you're leaving because you love them and yourself too much to stay and complain and breed resentment and contempt. I know it's counter-intuitive. I know this runs contrary to conventional wisdom. I know it may be unpopular, but it's possible that one of the most authentic ways for you to love where you are is to leave it.

Whatever you do, don't stay where you are and blame others for your misery. You'll never blame your way into a better future. You must take action. That action begins when you own where you are. If you're going to stay there, determine that you're going to make where you are better. If you can't do that for some reason or another, leave.

Own it. Fix it. Leave it.

That's how you love where you are—and I'm not just talking about geography now . . .

CHAPTER ELEVEN

WHY ME?

I have a secret, irrational fear. Psychologists call it Imposter Syndrome—a collection of feelings of inadequacy that persist even in the face of information that indicates the opposite to be true. It is experienced internally as chronic self-doubt and feelings of intellectual fraudulence. It is basically feeling that you're not really a successful, competent, and smart person—that you are only posing as such. No matter how much success you experience, you're never quite able to internalize it. It all must be due to luck or just being in the right place at the right time or your ability to charm and fool people.

I've got it, and I've got it bad.

The truth is, I've wrestled with it on and off for my entire life. I hear people say great things about me, but inside my head there's a little voice that whispers, "Yeah, but if they knew what you're really like, they'd say something else."

Recently, due to heightened stress, too little rest, physical pain, and a series of unwise choices, I have been consumed with this fear that at any moment someone is going to stand up, point their finger at me, and yell, "Imposter!"

Of course, I'll know they're talking about me and that the jig is up. I was able to fool them for a while, but in the end my incompetence will be discovered. I will be disgraced.

I know for a fact that my Facebook page has more than five thousand "likes." I know that I have nearly four thousand followers on Twitter. I've written several books—one that became a best-seller on Amazon—one that has been translated into multiple languages. I've been invited all over the planet to speak. I've had some success.

I also know that many of you reading these words are very successful people in your own right—writers, preachers, therapists, coaches, scholars, teachers, doctors, lawyers, business people. Some of you are probably more successful than I am. And I'm pretty sure that I'm not the only one of us who struggles with these irrational feelings of insecurity and inadequacy.

I wrestle with Imposter Syndrome. I am so afraid that if people really knew me—really knew the real me—the one who says terrible things to other drivers . . . to myself . . . to my kids . . . to my girlfriend . . . to people right after I hang up the phone—the one who does the wrong thing about as often as he does the right thing—if people knew that guy . . . well . . . they wouldn't like me very much.

And they might leave me alone.

And that's a terrifying idea for me to consider. I can't stand the thought of being cut off and excluded—of not being invited into the inner ring. I am afraid that people will not value me or respect me. I am desperate to be accepted and valued and loved! To be completely known and still completely embraced—that is what I long for.

And yet . . . on the one occasion when I think I actually got it, I managed to screw it up and throw it away. I think. I hope not, but that's what it looks like now.

I am desperate for two things: (1) someone who will love, accept, champion, and value me, and (2) the courage to say this out loud to others. So, that's what I'm doing here. I'm saying it right now.

I've been trying to live with more vulnerability of late, and I'm discovering something I never thought possible: Most people don't care. Most people don't care that I'm a mess. Most people don't care that my act isn't more together than it is. Most people don't care that I'm imperfect.

In fact, most people prefer me this way. Don't get me wrong. There are people who do care. There are people who care a great deal. There are people who do not want me to be broken or messed up. They don't want to hear about it. They liked me better when I was a pretender. They wanted an imposter. They got angry when I took off the mask.

Most of them have left by now.

The ones who remain, the ones who are showing me how to be an even better version of myself, have walked toward me in my mess, put their arms around me, and said, "Me, too." They know that I'm not as good as I can be yet. They know that I'm not as good as I often pretend to be. But they also know that I'm not through yet.

One of the ways the western world has changed drastically over the past five hundred years or so is in the way we view ourselves. The roots of this go back further in time. You could find them in Augustine's language, but they really took hold after the Protestant Reformation.

Christianity—arguably the greatest influence on Western civilization—has historically emphasized both the dignity and the depravity of human beings. During the Renaissance period, human dignity was overemphasized. Since then, our depravity has been where we've focused most of our attention. And this has led many people to be confused about how it is we ought to love ourselves. Should it be assumed? Or is it something we need to cultivate? Is it even appropriate?

Thomas Aquinas said, "Well-ordered self-love . . . is right and natural" (*The Summa Theologica* 1a.77.4 ad 1). But what is "well-ordered?" How do you define that? Who gets to say? I could go on and on discussing the historical development and the theology of all of this, but my main point is this: I'm not very good at loving myself—never have been—but I'm trying to get better at it.

WHO I AM RIGHT NOW

When I was younger, I was a bit of a wunderkind. I made good grades. I was athletically gifted. I was well-liked. I could sing. I was bright. I was busy. I did things well. I got attention. And I was ready to snap.

I was so ravenous for success and acceptance and approval that I would do just about anything to get it—even if it meant exhausting myself by pretending to be something I was not and overextending myself in an attempt to be everything I thought other people wanted me to be.

What's worse, I was never satisfied with myself or my accomplishments. I became a perfectionist. I was obsessed with getting better at things—and not in a healthy way. Run faster. Jump higher. Study longer. Sing louder. Work harder. Be better.

I beat myself up mercilessly. My internal dialogue was verbally abusive. All these years later . . . I'm a forty-seven-year-old man with grey hair and teenaged daughters. I've stopped playing sports. I haven't sung in public in years (outside of church or birthday parties). I haven't taken a class in a long time. And I still beat myself up on a daily basis.

> I tell lies for no good reason—something is wrong with me.
> I'm struggling to pay my bills right now—something is wrong with me.
> I have not lived up to my potential professionally or personally—something is wrong with me.
> I read all these self-improvement books, but I still struggle with the same, old stuff—something is wrong with me.

On and on it goes. The amount of evidence I present against myself in the courtroom of my mind is overwhelming, and it demonstrates—beyond a shadow of a reasonable doubt—that there is clearly something terribly wrong with me.

But I am going to say something right now what I have been working up the courage to say for decades. This is not an easy thing for me to say, and I may debate the veracity of this statement for a very long time. Still, I am going to say it because I think I need to say it somewhere, and here seems as good a place as any.

I'm alright.

Yes, I could stand to get better. But, no, I'm not that bad. I'm okay. Sometimes, I'm good. On rare occasions, I think I'm great. Mostly, I think I'm alright. I'm doing the best I can, and I'm trying (in healthy ways) to get a little bit better every day. I make a lot of mistakes, which means I'm gently pushing myself to grow and learn and do new things—things I'm not yet good at.

I am the only me there is and ever will be, and I am the only chance the world will ever have to know someone just like me. There is no such thing as the way I'm supposed to be. No one has ever been who I am, where I am, when I am before—so there's no manual for how I'm supposed to be other than the way I am right now. I'm not only becoming someone, I am someone right this moment. And who I am right now matters.

THE PERSON I'M BECOMING

Everyone lives as two people: the person you are right now and the person you are becoming. This is one of the things that makes finding love so tricky. For someone to really become your partner in life, they must accept both of those people—the person you are now and the person you are becoming. For much of my life, I was in relationships with people who liked who I was but not who I was becoming . . . or vice versa. The people who truly love me now must embrace both and must be willing to live with and walk with me as I try to navigate the gap between who I am and who I'm becoming.

I have been endowed with certain things by my Creator, and when he looks at me, he calls me his friend. I am not just tolerated; I am loved. I am cherished. I am adored—and not through gritted teeth. My Creator thinks I'm alright. He thinks I'm more than alright; he thinks I'm beautiful—flawed, but beautiful. I'm coming to believe he's right.

As you must have figured out by now, I'm big on self-improvement. I've read lots of self-help books, listened to lots of messages about how to be a better person, gone to conferences, invested in education, spoken with therapists. I am constantly trying to grow and learn and get better at being the me I was created to be.

And yet . . .

It's one thing to seek transformation for the sake of growth, improvement, and new horizons. It's another thing to feel so dissatisfied with yourself that no amount of growth can convince you that you're worthwhile and lovable. That kind of self-loathing has secretly characterized most of my life. It's like I've been trying to replace myself with someone better because I have never been and never will be good enough.

Ironically, I've taught all over the world the message of God's love and how it infuses each of us with value and dignity. But I have not always practiced what I have preached. Instead, I have been closed off to the idea that anyone—even God himself—could find me desirable.

Truth is, on most days, I keep a running tally of all thc ways I have screwed up. All the dumb things I said, stupid ideas I suggested, unsuccessful attempts to make people like me. All the bad things I've done. Times when I let people down. I keep it all up here in my head.

I wish I could say that this is all a "before" picture and that I can't even remember being that guy now. But this remains something I struggle with. I can say that I've spent the better part of the last few years taking two steps forward and one step back. Before then, it was often in reverse—one step forward and two steps back. But I am making progress. The fact that I'm brave enough to share this with you demonstrates that.

I think.

On a deeply primal level, I long to be loved, accepted, and celebrated. I'm learning that the foundation of true joy, however, is my own willingness and ability to love, accept, and celebrate myself. That's a really difficult thing for me to do when I . . .

- Consistently apologize for who I am as if I owe other people an explanation.
- Beat myself up when I make the slightest mistake.
- Obsess over my flaws and feel a sense of anger and disgust.

- Get clingy with people who see the best in me because I find it hard to maintain positive feelings when they're gone.
- Tell myself I'm being selfish when I practice simple, basic self-care.
- Repeatedly do destructive things that show I don't respect and value myself.
- Always find a reason to talk myself out of my dreams—as if maybe I don't deserve to have them.

I've done each and every one of these things at various points in my life. I'm guessing I'm not the only one. Sometimes loving myself is a challenge.

It's a beautiful thing to embrace growth and change—to recognize that I am not yet what I could be and work toward being the best me possible. But it's vitally important for me to remember that I am beautiful and wonderful right now.

IMPORTANT REMINDERS

In light of that, here are some things I'm reminding myself of these days.

1. I am not my worst mistakes. My past has shaped who I am, but I am not who I have been. I don't need to carry around labels or sins of the past as if they define me. Whatever I have done, it's done. It doesn't have to continue to brand me—especially if I'm making a conscious decision to do things differently now. For the record, I have done great things in my past, too. I can judge myself by my weakest moments or my strongest—that's my choice.

2. I have nothing to prove. Everyone has stuff in their past that they're proud of and stuff they're ashamed of. We all wish people would remember more of the former and less of the latter. We all want validation. We all feel alone sometimes. We often feel alone because we believe we haven't proved our worth. But I don't have to show the world that I'm enough. I don't have to try to hide the things I've done that might seem terrible. My Creator offers me forgiveness. Now I need to forgive and accept myself and trust that other people will as well.

Being authentic requires vulnerability—allowing others to see me and trusting that they won't judge me, and knowing that if/when they do, that says way more about them than it does about me. I'm going to be real. Those who accept me will accept me fully. I will not pretend and then have to maintain the illusion that I am something I'm not.

3. The dark stuff is important. I have made mistakes. Who hasn't? The beautiful part of having fallen is that I am in a position now to help others with the same experience. I know what it feels like to fall. I know that hurt. I also know what it feels like to receive grace and mercy, to look up and see someone with their hand extended, not to strike me in anger but to help pull me out of the pit I dug for myself. Now I can reach out and help other people up when they need it. When I realize that my failings can help heal the world, they seem less like liabilities and more like assets.

4. I matter. When I was in elementary school, an authority figure in my life said, "If I were one of your classmates, I wouldn't be your friend." I believed him, and for years I carried that around with me. I believed that, given the choice, most people wouldn't like me. As I got older, a lot of people seemed uncomfortable around me, and I could never quite figure out why. As I look back, I realize I was so clingy and needy. I so desperately wanted someone to un-say that one terrible thing someone had spoken so many years ago. I could not believe I mattered until someone said it to me. I know now that I do matter. I touch people's lives every day—even if they don't mention it on social media. The things I do have a ripple effect that I'll never be able to measure. It may not change my Klout score, but the smallest act of love is important because it can grow.

5. My positive feelings and actions create more positive feelings and actions. All these warm fuzzies won't matter if they never prompt me to get out into the world—not to do the things I think others think I should do, but to do the things I really want to do. To do that thing that scares the spit out of me, that thing that excites me beyond measure. I'm giving myself permission to do things, even if they're not always perfect, to focus on progress instead of perfection. I'm allowing myself to be kind to myself and to others and to the world.

Of course, I have room for improvement, but my weaknesses will not define me. I will not worry about the future. I will not dwell in the past. I will remember that I deserve to enjoy the present, but I recognize that only I can make that happen.

I haven't always been good at this. I've let a lot of time pass when I retreated into the confines of my own mind, wishing to be someone better than who I am. But right now, I'm happy with me.

MAKING A LIST

This has been awkward for me to write. I feel like I've split myself open and allowed you to see something you may recoil from in horror. I'm flawed—like we all are—and that's not only okay, I think it's beautiful.

A few summers ago, a guy in a white coat gave it to me straight: "There's cancerous activity in your esophagus." It's hard to explain this, but I actually felt a little good about hearing that news. The diagnosis made my inner hypochondriac feel so vindicated! I always knew something would be wrong with me. Now I had a professional agreeing with me.

I ended up taking plenty of drugs, submitting to tests and therapy, and, despite all this stress and my poor dietary habits, there is actually no cancer there now—make of that what you will. So, I am not dead yet. And, until I am, I have decided to be fully alive. I am not content anymore merely to continue breathing; I want to really live the adventure that life can be. And it started with a list.

One morning after the doctors had tried unsuccessfully to execute a trans-nasal endoscopy, I slumped into the chair in my office and pulled out a yellow legal pad. At the top, I wrote the words "The List" and proceeded to write anything and everything that came to mind about what made life so amazing and so worth living. Before I knew it, my list was long—like more than a hundred things.

When I went back to read what I had written, a few things stood out. First, food was everywhere. Gary Chu's Martini Prawns from Osake in Santa Rosa, California. The Wiseguy at Pizzeria Bianco in Phoenix, Arizona. A double-double from In-n-Out. The chopped pork sandwich served Pittsburgh Style at 'Cue near my house. Really good sushi. Fresh pineapple. Cheese. The fact that "cheese" made the list before "mom" is probably something I should talk with my therapist about, but food was everywhere on my list of things that make life awesome.

Don't get me wrong, the people in my life certainly showed up. My daughters. My parents. My sister. Cousins. Aunts. Uncles. Friends. Mentors. Colleagues. My partner in crime. Names filled the list. But what surprised me most was how much of the list contained simple things:

- Autumn leaves
- The sound of Miles Davis's trumpet on "Kind of Blue"
- The smell of a fire
- Slow-dancing

- A well-written sentence
- Sunsets at the beach
- A good conversation

In our constant desire to reach the next plateau, my list seemed quiet. Staring in the eye what I thought could be death, I wasn't worried about getting a bigger house, more money, or a more impressive job title. I longed for simple, everyday things with the people I love.

Of course, this revelation is hardly extraordinary. Since the beginning of time, wise people have known the virtue of living in the now and appreciating the little things. Buddhists speak of Right Mindfulness: the practice of being present and paying attention to the situation at hand.

The Greek poet Horace reminded us to *carpe diem*—seize the day and pay no mind to the uncertainty of tomorrow. Jesus suggested we could all learn a lesson by observing how the birds and the flowers do not worry and yet flourish and thrive. Thoreau wanted to "live deep and suck out all the marrow of life." He said, "You must live in the present, launch yourself on every wave, find your eternity in each moment."

Even nine-hundred-year-old Yoda chided young Master Luke for having his head in the clouds. "All his life he looked away . . . to the future, to the horizon," the Jedi Master scolded. "Never his mind on where he was. Hmm? What he was doing. Hmph."

Ironically, a growing body of research backs up all that wisdom. For example, Harvard University developed an iPhone app to track the happiness levels of its participants at random intervals. The volunteers would reply with information about what they had just been focused on and how happy they felt.

The results? People are happiest when they are simply living in the moment and focused on what they are doing.

Other research shows that learning to savor small, positive moments can significantly increase your happiness and that people who foster an "attitude of gratitude" for everyday activities sleep better, are in better physical health, and have lower stress levels. Whether it's fantasizing about the weekend, rehashing an argument you had last week, or burying your head in your iPhone, it's easy to find ourselves everywhere but the here and now.

Furthermore, in our future-obsessed culture, we tend to look at achievements down the road as the key to ultimate fulfillment.

I'll be happy when I get married.

I'll be happy when I make $100,000.

I'll be happy when I have ten thousand followers on Twitter.

We're so preoccupied with the destination that we forget about the joy in the journey, the adventure of getting there.

I know. I know. Goals are important. They inspire us to be better, to try harder, to reach new heights. But there's a lot of joy and satisfaction to be found in the simple things. Embracing this may be the best way to find happiness on a regular basis.

This, of course, is easier said than done. Trust me. I know. I caught myself obsessing over this chapter while I should have been enjoying time with my daughters.

But I'm getting better.

I'm on a journey—sometimes I think it's a Homeric journey; other times I think it's more Abrahamic. And while it has been a difficult couple of years since I wrote that list, it's been an enlightening time as well. I've learned not to pin my hopes for happiness on something just over the horizon. I'm learning to live in the right now and embrace the simple pleasures like coffee and toast with strawberry jam.

I'm not dead yet. Until I am, I intend to live.

CHAPTER TWELVE

JESUS LOVES ME

Mark records a story for us. He writes, "A man with leprosy came to [Jesus] and begged him on his knees, 'If you are willing, you can make me clean'" (Mark 1:40).

You probably already know how leprosy was viewed by people during Jesus's time. In fact, most of us would still want to completely avoid someone with leprosy—even in our day of modern medicine. Back then, though, it was worse—way worse. Back then, leprosy wasn't just a medical condition; there was a moral stigma attached to it as well.

People thought that if you had leprosy, you'd probably done something to deserve it. After all, God wouldn't let a good person catch leprosy, would he? Lepers weren't just required to announce that they were sick; they had to announce that they were "unclean." Lepers weren't ill; they were dirty.

Rabbis taught that if a leper got close enough to be hit with a stone, he should be pelted until he ran a safe distance away. Sin and suffering were contagious, after all. Get near enough to a person with leprosy—or a tax collector—or a prostitute—and their bad mojo might rub off on you. Better to keep away from all of them. Better to play it safe and maintain your own purity.

In other words, they practiced a strategy of isolation. The holier a person was (or wanted to be), the more unapproachable they became.

Lots of people in lots of churches and lots of Christian families still practice this strategy today. My local Christian radio station's motto is "Safe for the whole family." What exactly does that mean? It could mean, "We don't curse or tell dirty jokes on here." Or it could mean something else, something less than Christlike. It could mean, "On here we're free from all those pesky outsiders. Sequestered. Insulated. Quarantined. Unsavory characters aren't allowed on here, and we like it that way."

And that makes what happens next in this story of Jesus and the leper so shocking. Mark continues, "Jesus was indignant. He reached out his hand and touched the man. 'I am willing,' he said. 'Be clean!' Immediately the leprosy left him and he was cleansed" (v. 41–42).

Think of it. Jesus was the holiest man who ever lived. Never did one thing wrong. Never had an evil motive. Never told a lie. Never entertained an impure thought. Sure, he struggled with temptation, but he never once gave in. He was the holiest, most righteous man of all time.

But no one heard any holier-than-thou-ness from him. You will not find a trace of self-righteousness in Jesus's conversations. Instead, you find him to be the most approachable man you could ever imagine. Lepers, IRS agents, hookers, lawyers, teachers, divorcées, men, women, soldiers, children—people of all shapes and sizes and colors flocked to him. Terribly worldly people felt totally comfortable having him at their parties.

But most of the same kinds of people who ran *to* Jesus now run *from* his followers. Something's gone terribly wrong. Sinners received compassion from Jesus; too often they receive a stern, judgmental lecture from us.

The leper in the story didn't doubt Jesus's ability to help. He knew that Jesus was capable. He wondered whether or not Jesus would be willing to do something for someone like him. How many lost and hurting people today keep their distance from Jesus because of the deep and profound shame they feel? How many stay at arm's length from the Compassionate One because they think they are unworthy to meet him face-to-face?

I know I have.

Jesus is willing. Jesus, the Approachable One, invites all who desire to come close. We need not be afraid. I don't have to clean myself up first. I couldn't if I tried. He invites me to come just as I am. He even does something unthinkable. He reaches for me before I reach for him.

Look back at the story. Jesus touched the leper. He reached out his hand and touched the man before he healed him. This was, technically, against the Law (see Leviticus). That's got to be hard to read if you're a legalist. But Jesus was willing and able to touch the leper because he knew something no one else seemed to know.

Jesus knew that leprosy is not the only thing that's contagious. Sin and suffering spread, but so do love and joy and laughter.

The leper didn't infect Jesus; Jesus infected him. What was in Jesus was simply stronger than what was in the leper. Maybe this is what the Apostle John had in mind when he wrote, "The one who is in you is greater than the one who is in the world" (1 John 4:4). That leper was more contagious after his encounter with Jesus than he was before he was healed or cleansed or whatever.

So, who's the leper in your world? Who's the person you keep your distance from? Their sin is too bad, too contagious. You don't even want to get close to that person lest you should catch what it is they've got.

Maybe one reason we aren't as approachable as Jesus is because we don't really have anything that contagious. If so, let's admit it. They're not the ones with the problem; we are. And our biggest problem may be the fact that we've never seen ourselves as the leper in the story.

But me? I know. I have leprosy. I'm gross. That's not the whole truth about me, but it's part of it. Until I'm willing to be the leper, I don't have a chance of ever being touched, of being cleansed, of being made whole again. And I'll never have anything truly worth catching.

SHINING THE LIGHT ON NICK AT NIGHT

Nicodemus was a member of the upper echelon of Jewish society. He was wealthy, educated, and well-respected. He was part of a group that was responsible for making sure the Jewish people were happy with the Romans and the Romans were happy with the Jewish people. As long as they did their job, the Romans made life very comfortable for them. So, the name of the game was "Don't Rock the Boat."

Only one person was allowed to rock the boat as far as the Jewish ruling council was concerned: The Messiah. He could rock as hard as he wanted, because they knew he would drive the Romans out and return Israel to its rightful place of international prominence. When the Messiah showed up, they knew he would set things right (with all his might), and they would thrive in his kingdom much more than they had in the Roman domain.

When Nicodemus showed up to talk to Jesus, he wanted to know if Jesus had any inside information on when God might actually show up and initiate this kingdom. But he didn't actually get around to asking about that. Instead, he started: "Rabbi, we know that you are a teacher who has come from God. For no one could perform the signs you are doing if God were not with him" (John 3:2). He had planned this out, surely, and was about to go on.

Jesus kind of interrupted him. "Very truly I tell you, no one can see the kingdom of God unless they are born again" (v. 3).

Nicodemus must have thought Jesus was joking. Born again? Nicodemus (like most other Jewish men) thought he'd been born right the first time. He didn't need to be born again. He was already a Jewish man. It didn't get any better than that.

What Jesus was saying to Nicodemus was so different from what Nick and his friends believed that it must have really taken him off guard. Jesus was saying that God was not a racist, that being related to the right people doesn't get you into God's kingdom.

The Pharisees of Jesus's day (and of our day as well) believed that entrance into God's kingdom is based on being born the right way and living the right way. Be Jewish and obey the Law. That's how you get in, and that's how you stay in. There's a good God who only lets good people into his good kingdom.

Jesus says that's wrong. Good people don't get into the kingdom; forgiven people do. This came as quite a shock to the people Jesus encountered. (And there are people today who still refuse to believe it). This is really confusing to some—offensive, frightening, disorienting. But if you'll stay there in the light for a while, your eyes will adjust, and you'll be able to see how great this arrangement really is.

You'll also see how you don't deserve it any more than anyone else does.

EQUAL OPPORTUNITY SAVIOR

The only thing more conspicuous than a woman going to get water from a well at high noon would be a Jewish rabbi deigning to talk to a Samaritan woman (at a well at high noon) who had been married several times and was currently shacked up with a guy. But that's exactly what we find in John 4, and it gets even stranger! Jesus asks her for a drink, but she notices he doesn't have anything to draw water with—no cup, no bucket, nothing. Does he intend to drink from her water jar?

Doesn't he know how gross that would be?! She's a Samaritan woman, living in sin. She might as well be wearing a scarlet "A" right across her chest. You couldn't get any further "outside" for a typical Jewish rabbi.

Ah, but Jesus is always far from typical.

The story of the Samaritan woman at the well is remarkable on its own merits. But when we read it alongside John's previous chapter—the bit where Jesus has his encounter with Nicodemus—it's earth shattering. Here's the Messiah who comes to the upper-uppers and the lower-lowers, the high and mighty as well as the down and out. Men and women, wealthy and poor, moral and immoral, proud and ashamed—no matter where you've been or what you've been up to, Jesus, the Equal Opportunity Savior, comes for you.

Some people have a hard time believing he came for people like them. Other people have a hard time believing he came for people unlike them. When you remember that he comes for all, it's easier to go into the world and mingle with folks you wouldn't otherwise associate with.

WHY HE HAD TO GO THERE

She had baggage. There was no avoiding that. She'd been married five times and was now living with a man she was not married to. That's odd in our times. We can only imagine how deviant it must have seemed to people two thousand years ago.

We don't know why she'd had five different husbands. Maybe they all died. Maybe they all left her. Maybe she left some of them, and some of them left her, and one of them died. We don't know, but there are several combinations, and they all lead to the same outcome. She'd had her heart broken more than once.

It's important to remember that once upon a time, she was a little girl. She had dreams. She had hopes. She thought about what it would be like to get married, what she would wear that day, whom would be invited, what the party would be like, how long it would last. She may have played that scenario out in her mind as the day drew closer and closer. I doubt very seriously that she ever stopped to think that it might not last forever.

The end of a marriage is like a death in the family. Nothing prepares a person for it. And, to some extent, it doesn't matter whose fault it is; when a marriage ends, more than one heart breaks. Maybe it was her fault—maybe it wasn't—maybe it wasn't anyone's fault—maybe it just happened. Regardless, when it ended, she must have been devastated.

Now, can you imagine what she must have thought and felt when someone—after what was considered a proper amount of time had passed—asked her to do it again?

"I know your first marriage didn't end up the way you had hoped, but would you marry me?"

Maybe she jumped at it and said, "Sure!" Or maybe she thought she wasn't ready. Maybe she felt the icy grip of fear clutch her throat. Maybe every fiber of her being screamed out how there was no way in the world she would ever put herself in a position to go through that nightmarish hell again.

But somehow, she managed to wrestle down the fear, put her past behind her, and get on with her life. So she said, "Yes."

And how long was it before her worst possible case scenario began to play out in front of her very eyes?

It happened again. And again. And again. And again.

Was it a matter of survival? Was her father dead, and marrying was the only way to avoid homelessness and having to beg for alms at the city gate? We don't know. What we do know is that five times she gave her heart away. Five times she'd had it broken. When Jesus finds her, she's only willing to go halfway—she lives with a guy, but they're not married. Angry? Bitter? Frustrated? Probably. Thirsty? No doubt.

Now you know why the Bible says, Jesus "had to go through Samaria" (John 4:4). See, Jesus wasn't content to just be approachable. I mean, sure, he was probably glad to know that people felt like they could just walk up to him and ask him whatever was on their minds, whatever they wanted to know but were confused about God, about life here on earth, about what happens after life here on earth.

But Jesus didn't just sit back and say, "Well, I'm here. They know where I am. If they want to talk, they can come to me." Jesus wasn't just approachable. Jesus approached.

WHEN I GROW UP

Not too long ago, someone asked me what I want to be when I finally grow up. They weren't trying to be condescending; they were just pointing out the fact that I don't have much of a "real job." I bounce around here and there as an itinerant kind of guy. I don't have an expense account or a company car. I don't always have a regular paycheck.

Don't get me wrong. I make a living. Sometimes I squeak by, other times I have plenty of margin. I have a job. It just doesn't look like anything you'd call "normal."

When I was a kid, for a while I wanted to be a policeman. I also wanted to be a trash collector because I thought they only worked on Tuesdays. I wanted to be a professional baseball player or a professional football player. I never once thought, "I'd like to grow up and work for the IRS."

In fact, I've never heard anyone say, "Working for the Internal Revenue Service has been a lifelong dream of mine since childhood."

Doctors. Nurses. Astronauts. Firemen. Veterinarians. Rock Stars. Rodeo Clowns. Yes.

IRS agent? No.

In ancient Israel, certain jobs were not just distasteful; they were downright despicable. In fact, some rabbis actually maintained a list of jobs that were unacceptable. For example, physicians and butchers were considered socially despised trades, because they were constantly handling blood and guts, and they generally showed special treatment to wealthy people.

Tanners and dung collectors also made the list—for obvious reasons. There was even a special dispensation for women whose husbands became dung collectors. They could divorce their husbands with none of the normal social and religious repercussions.

Then there was a completely different category of jobs that were actually considered immoral. Merely taking one of these jobs was considered a sin, an affront to God and the nation. People who gambled with dice. People who were involved in usury (lending money to people). Pigeon trainers (pigeon racing was a common form of gambling at the time).

At the bottom of the list: Tax Collector.

It's hard to overstate just how deep the hatred ran toward people who earned their living collecting taxes. They were not only avoided and despised, they also were deprived of many of their civil rights. They weren't allowed to testify in court. They weren't allowed to serve as judges or elders. A devout Israelite wouldn't even allow the hem of his robe to brush up against the robe of a tax collector.

All of this background makes what Jesus did in Luke 19 so remarkable. Jesus encountered a little man named Zacchaeus, who had climbed up in a sycamore tree. Zacchaeus wasn't just a tax collector; he was "a chief tax collector" (v. 2). This means he had ascended through the ranks of the other run-of-the-mill tax collectors and had distinguished himself as one of the best tax collectors around. Most Jewish people would have viewed him as one of the worst people in the world.

But something about Jesus made the worst people in the world think there might actually be some kind of hope, even for them. Jesus was obviously from God. Like Nicodemus had pointed out, all you had to do was look at all the miracles he did. But Jesus hung out with people who seemed an awful lot like Zacchaeus.

Still, the little man wasn't sure he wanted to get too close. He wanted to see Jesus, but he also wanted to be able to keep a safe distance. That's one reason he climbed a tree—he wanted to see without being seen.

And he probably thought his plan was going to work. Jesus came right up next to the tree, and Zach was probably thinking, "This is great. I can see him. I'm going to be able to hear every word he says." But then Jesus stopped and actually looked up into the tree. Now, the plan had backfired. There was no escape. Jesus had the little man up a tree.

"Zacchaeus, come down immediately" (v. 5).

Notice that Jesus did not say, "Zacchaeus, don't make me come up there!" Nor did he say, "Peter? John? Go up there and get him!"

Jesus invited Zacchaeus to come down, and then it was his choice. Zacchaeus could have stayed up there. He could have held on for dear life, and Jesus would have probably gone away eventually. But then there would have been no healing, no restoration.

The first step is always this: Will you come out of hiding? Until you do, there can be no real community, no real intimacy with God or others. Unless you're willing to come out of hiding, you'll be forever stuck up a tree.

But, if Jesus's patience is astonishing (and it is), there's something he's about to say that's even more breathtaking. Jesus looks up into the tree and says to this man who is despised and shunned by his own people, "Zacchaeus, come down immediately. I must stay at your house today."

Not, "Come down here so I can give you the thrashing you've got coming." Not, "Come down here and apologize for what you've been doing to these nice people."

"Come down immediately. I must stay at your house today."

Not, "I want to." Not, "I'm going to."

"I must."

I read other stories, and I root for Jesus. I want him to reach out and touch the leper. I want him to heal that man who was born blind. I can identify with those guys. Neither of them did anything to deserve their situation.

I want Jesus to explain things to Nicodemus. He seems to be a good guy with a good heart—kind of like me. He just has some misguided beliefs and bad theology to work through. He's been blinded to the truth, but if someone will just explain it to him in language he can understand, I'm sure he'll come around.

When Jesus goes out of his way to call out Zacchaeus, though, there's something in me that cringes. This guy has chosen his situation. Nobody forced him to become a tax collector. He brought this upon himself. He knew the right thing, and he chose to do wrong anyway.

And that sounds like the me I don't like to admit to being.

Still, Jesus says, "This is what I must do. My mission will be incomplete unless I go to your house today."

This is how grace is revealed. This is how the Kingdom of God breaks into our world. This is the work of God—not some kind of distraction from it.

Jesus came to show kindness to people who would never receive it elsewhere. He came to offer acceptance to people who did not deserve it. He came to bring grace and mercy to sinful little people like you and me and Zacchaeus.

Jesus says, "I must." He must offer acceptance, community, and fellowship to those on the outside—even those who have done it on purpose!

Jesus says, "I must." And, as one who claims to follow him, I must do these things as well. I must go and find those whose lives are in shambles through no fault of their own. I must go and find those who are mistaken in their thinking and blind to the truth. But I must also go and find those who have chosen to do wrong even though they knew better. And I must offer grace and healing to them too.

I must do these things because it forces me to acknowledge the fact that I am those people, too. I am the guy in the ditch, the man born blind, the pious know-it-all Pharisee, the leper, the tax collector, the woman at the well, the one caught in adultery, the thief on the cross. I denied Jesus with Peter. Like Paul, I am the chief of sinners.

When I finally manage to grow up, I don't intend to be the next Billy Graham or Rick Warren. I don't need to get a job that pays gobs of money and provides me with the kind of security most people have. Those things are nice and all, but I've set my sights way higher than that.

As cheesy as it sounds, when I grow up, I want to be like Jesus. I want to see people the way he sees them and be open for them to come see me too. I want to love as Jesus did. I want his love to permeate me to the point that I leak it everywhere I go. I don't just want to love other people, I want to be love-wrapped-in-skin standing in their midst. I don't want to have love or show love; I want to be love.

In order to do that, I have to let Jesus love me. In order to do that, I have to stop trying to earn his love, trying to pay him back, trying to give him a good reason so that he won't feel like he got ripped off in this bargain. I have to surrender to it. I have to sit still and let him love me.

Jesus loves me, this I know, for the Bible tells me so. Little ones to him belong. They are weak, but he is strong.

Yes, Jesus loves me.

Yes, Jesus loves me.

Yes, Jesus loves me.

The Bible tells me so.

Now, if only I could learn to rest in that.

CHAPTER THIRTEEN

MORE OF HIM AND MORE OF ME

When I was a kid, growing up and singing hymns in the church where my father preached, we frequently sang "None of Self and All of Thee," written by a Frenchman named Theodore Monod in 1875. It began with a shameful look at self. They don't write songs for worship like this anymore.

Oh, the bitter pain and sorrow
That a time could ever be,
When I proudly said to Jesus,
"All of self, and none of Thee."

Then, with each passing stanza, the song suggested a growing change of heart that finally culminated in a triumphant heart-felt transformation:

Higher than the highest heaven,
Deeper than the deepest sea,
Lord, Thy love at last has conquered:
"None of self, and all of Thee."

Obviously, the sentiment here comes from John the Baptist who famously said, "He must become greater; I must become less" (John 3:30). This is said to be one of the reasons why the ancient church set John's birthday near the summer solstice, the day when the hours of daylight in the northern hemisphere begin to recede. John, like the sunlight, had to diminish so Jesus could rise to his position of preeminence. As John fades into the background, Jesus can finally take his rightful place at the front and center of what God is doing among the Jewish people.

I was taught as a child that this was a metaphor for me and my personality. The less of me I could let show through, the more Christ in me could be seen. The objective is to cover myself up. After all, I'm flawed and warty. Jesus is beautiful and radiant. He's all that matters. The best I can hope for is to merely be a vessel to carry Jesus into the world. I don't matter. He does. In fact, it might be better if I were totally invisible. None of self, and all of Thee.

I have a friend I really do love. He lives with such an incredibly high level of integrity, and he's such an authentic and bold man of God. I always leave his presence feeling better about myself and about the world. We have fun. He has a great sense of humor. I just love him.

We frequently find ourselves speaking at the same events—a conference here or a lectureship there. And sometimes, because he's so highly respected, he gets called upon to pray for all the speakers. His prayers are deep and rich. It's obvious he spends a lot time talking to God. But at these events, he frequently ends his prayers by asking God to remove us from the equation, for God to let the people listening forget that we're even there. He asks God to make the speakers like a piece of glass, transparent, so that those listening will just see Jesus shining through us, and nothing of us will leave any kind of impression at all.

The first time I remember him praying that over me, I thought, "This guy is deep. I never would have thought to pray something like that. I must have a gigantic ego." But now I've totally changed my mind. While my friend has a noble idea, I think his prayer is totally off base and, worse, it might be blasphemous.

Here's why: God doesn't want me to disappear. He doesn't want to give me a personality transplant. God wants to use me, with my bent, my leanings, my vocabulary, my experiences. God wants me to be me.

JESUS AND ME

We have four different accounts of the life of Jesus recorded for us in our Bibles. Four different men, with four different backgrounds, using four different perspectives to tell the same story to four different audiences. Peter's letters read differently from Paul's or John's. God never says to Isaiah, "You know, I really wish you were more like Jeremiah."

Yes, in one sense we're all in the process of becoming more like Jesus, but this doesn't necessarily mean we're all in the process of becoming more similar to one another. It's not like the Borg, where we will all be assimilated into one collective consciousness with no more distinction of persona or personality. Jesus in me is going to look different from Jesus in you. We're not going to end up looking and thinking and speaking in monotone unison. Harmony suffers when all we do is try to sound like one voice.

Somehow, the mystery of transformation lies in the fact that while I am becoming a whole new me, I'm also becoming a more potent version of the me I already am, the me I've been all along. The me I am when I'm in my right mind—when I'm "in the zone"—me without all the junk and baggage I've managed to accumulate over the past forty-seven years but with all the wisdom and knowledge and perspective the junk and baggage can give me.

It's not none of self and more of Thee; it's more of self and more of Thee. Somehow, in the alchemy of God's kingdom, the more like Jesus I become, the more myself I also become.

My dad used to use this illustration while preaching. It was based on a television commercial from Hertz rental cars. They would show a car, and a person would be scooped up into the air by some unseen force and dropped behind the wheel of the car. Then the voiceover would say, "Let Hertz put you in the driver's seat."

My dad would repeat that phrase and then say, "God wants to take you out of the driver's seat."

God is, without a doubt, the most frustrating person I've ever met in my life. From my dad's illustration, I got the idea that following Jesus would get easier as I got older. I could not have been more wrong. Secretly, I thought that one day Jesus would flag me down while I was driving my car. He would tell me to scoot over, and he would take over driving. While Jesus chauffeured me around, I would sit in back in the passenger seat and wave at all my friends as we drove past, enjoying the scenery and fiddling with the radio. Jesus could make all the driving decisions, as long as he was steering me safely home.

Admittedly, I'm a bit of a control freak, and it might take a while to adjust to not being behind the wheel. But Jesus would drive me wherever he wanted me to go, and I would learn to live with it.

I've learned as I get older that Jesus asks me to do something far more difficult than let him drive. He flags down my car and says, "Follow me." Then he goes to get in his own car. He has not given me good directions (and sometimes no directions at all).

He's not really interested in giving me guidance; he wants to be my guide.

Now, some people are easy to follow. They drive the speed limit, slow down at intersections, use their turn signals, and brake early. Jesus is not like that; he blows through yellow lights and makes kamikaze lane changes. He may even try a left turn from the right-hand lane. Following Jesus is not relaxing. It's the most exhausting, nerve-wracking, nail-biting experience imaginable.

But this is what I am called to do: follow him. I don't have much of a map. I have a vague, general idea of where I'm going, but mostly I'm just trying to stay as close to his back bumper as I can. And when I finally get where I'm going, I'll know I couldn't have done it on my own. The only way I'll get where I need to go is by paying attention to the man in front of me.

That's what following Jesus means, and I'm supposed to stay on high alert because he could make a hard right at any moment. He doesn't always feel the need to signal. I may have to run a few red lights just to keep up. I may end up having to make a U-turn and find him again. But that's following Jesus; there's not really a pattern to it.

God's plan for my life often seems to come out of left field. Any relationship with God, any attempt to study his character and nature, will and should confound our expectations. This is the strangeness of God, the left-handedness. It's not the priest who saves the guy in the ditch; it's the filthy Samaritan. It's not the oldest or the tallest who becomes king; it was the runt of the litter, David. The chosen people are named after a heel-grabbing con man and trickster. The disciples aren't the best and brightest; most were uneducated, blue-collar, working-class stiffs, a tax agent, and one even has ties to a terrorist organization. Jesus himself does not save us through military victory but through suffering death on a cross.

Throughout the Bible, you find God doing the unexpected. He uses the guy whose right hand is withered. The last are first. The servant of all is the greatest of all. The smart look dumb, and the foolish become wise. The proud are humbled, and the humble are exalted. Heroes are shown to be embarrassingly human. Enemy number one of the church ends up being its greatest evangelist. It's not as if these stories are tucked away in the unusual corners of the text; they're everywhere. They're not the exception; they're the rule. Sometimes it's ten plagues; sometimes it's ten commandments.

Or the death of the firstborn. Or a virgin birth. Ultimately, it's an execution that leads to a resurrection.

And so my childhood idea that one day God's love would win me over to the point where I could say, "None of self, and all of Thee," is confounded by the fact that this is never what actually happens in the Bible. Instead, God uses people and makes them fully themselves—more themselves than they were before they collided with Jesus in the first place. Dallas Willard put it this way in the *Divine Conspiracy*: "I am learning from Jesus to live my life as he would live *my* life if he were [me]. I am not necessarily learning to do everything he did, but I am learning how to do everything I do in the manner that he did all that he did" (283).

Also, while we're on the topic of God doing things in bizarre, unpredictable, left-handed sorts of ways, here's the biggest surprise of all. While I've been spending all this time fretting and kvetching about the fact that I'm still me after all the effort I've put in to trying to change myself, I find out that when I get good and fed up with trying and just sit still, transformation has a way of finding me.

Imagine that. When I try to change, I'm still me. When I still me, I change.

ME AND PETER'S MESSAGE ABOUT LIFE

When I was about seven years old, Steve Martin released his comedy album, *Let's Get Small*. That's the one that has "Excuse Me" on it. If you're close to my age, you surely know what I'm talking about. I had large sections of this record memorized. I could probably do bits of it verbatim right now. I won't. But I probably could.

I was also an anxious child—which explains why I am such an anxious adult. I would lie in bed at night—blissfully unaware of just how much of a drug reference the "Let's Get Small" bit was—and think about it. What if there was something you could swallow that made you small? A potion you could drink like Alice did in Wonderland? I would obsess over this. I even began to feel it sometimes.

It would happen when I was still and quiet for a few minutes. I'd be standing in the outfield playing baseball in the vacant lot in my neighborhood. Or fishing from the banks of the man-made lake in our neighborhood. Or I'd be lying in my bed at night, drifting into the ether. And it would strike!

I would have the distinct impression that I was shrinking, growing smaller and smaller and smaller. My body would grow taut and rigid, and my eyes would squint tightly shut. My consciousness would float above my body, hovering near the ceiling of my bedroom. I could see my tiny self down there in a ridiculously over-sized bed with gigantic furniture. Lamps and chairs and bookshelves were enormous. The whole world had grown, and I had shrunk.

And then it would end.

Who knows how long the sensation would last. Maybe ten seconds. Maybe ten minutes. I couldn't make it happen; it happened to me. Honestly, I never tried to fight it, but I was never really excited when it happened. I never have understood what this was. Some sort of flaw in my design I suppose. A glitch in the system. I outgrew it. I can't remember the last time it happened.

But I kind of wish it would—if not physically, then metaphysically. I wish I could shrink—that I could lose everything that isn't essential, shed everything that's not part of my core, be reduced to my bare minimums. Discover the John inside of John that makes John, John.

I've written several books, and they're all preoccupied with the question of how to align myself with the purpose I was created for. How do I become the me I'm supposed to be? What should I start doing? What should I stop doing? What recipe of work and rest, discipline and play, study and laughter is required for me to emerge from the cocoon as the butterfly I'm meant to be? What needs to die so I can live? What needs to be fed more so I can be strong where I have been weak?

As a theologian, I've spent time studying the great Old Testament characters: Abraham, Jacob, Joseph, Moses, Joshua, Deborah, David, Esther, Solomon. I've spent time scrutinizing Jesus and Paul. You know who I've never had much time for? Peter. I'm not sure why. I never found him that interesting. Lovable perhaps—in that bumbling, oh-dear-what-did-he-say-now? sort of way. But I never thought he was that compelling as a thinker or a writer.

But that guy lived for three years with Jesus, shoulder-to-shoulder in the trenches, up close and personal. And then he helped Mark write his Gospel. And then he wrote two letters of his own that have been preserved for us. It's right at the top of the second letter that Peter says something that recently floored me.

Peter wrote that Jesus's "divine power has given us everything we need for a godly life" (2 Pet. 1:3). Everything. You don't need anything more. Everything you need for life (the Greek word is *zoe*, abundant existence overflowing out of your ears) and godliness (the Greek word is *eusebeia*, a real, true, vital, spiritual connection to your Creator) is available.

The life I've always wanted is available to me right now. Not next year. Not after I get through this particularly difficult season. Not when I've learned the lessons my forties are supposed to teach me. Not when my kids are grown and gone. Not after I see my therapist a few more times.

Right now, I have everything I need to have a life of abundance lived in close connection with my Creator. It's available to me right now. Of course, for me to receive this, I must first humble myself enough to ask for it. And receiving it as a gift means I can never claim to have earned it. It has so much of an upside, but it begins with the downside of me recognizing that I can't do it on my own.

Ironically, I can only get bigger when I make myself small. I can only get ahead when I allow myself to fall behind. I can only make progress when I make myself still.

NOT WHO I ONCE WAS

A funny thing happened during the process of working on this book: I turned into a whole different person. And it was excruciating. When I first started jotting down some of the ideas you've just read, my family was living outside of Dallas, Texas. I pastored a church that was growing. But I was miserable. We moved back to our nice, quiet house just outside of Atlanta, Georgia, and I kept plugging away at the ideas. I wrote a different book in the meantime, but I could never quite get away from the central thesis that I am not as far along as I figured I'd be by this point in time.

All my life I've wanted to be different, to be better than I am, to improve. But it intensified in my forties until it became nearly unbearable. As I got older, my shortcomings came into clearer view until they became almost all I could see. I began to detest them. To make matters worse, I began to wonder if I had been sold a bill of goods in my high school youth group. I had been told that God would honor my commitment to him and answer my fervent prayers.

But something happened on the way to heaven. I had gone to California to plant a church that folded within a year. I remember loading up the girls and the dog and driving out of our fair city, making our way westward, chasing the dream of building a new kind of church in southern California. We were so sure and so optimistic and so hopeful. But things don't always turn out the way you want.

It was a humbling experience in many ways. So many things unrealized, so many dreams left unfulfilled. I did my best to mask my disappointment (sometimes succeeding, probably failing more often than not), trying to hide from my kids the embarrassment and feelings of failure I experienced. It was hard not to feel like I was coming back with my tail tucked between my legs, a defeated man, a failed church planter, an extremely sinful one at that.

Being a writer is a solitary occupation, and that solitude doesn't do much to help those feelings of failure and alienation. Then I went to Texas and met with personal disaster. I probably shouldn't have gone so soon after the California debacle. I should have spent more time thinking, more time listening, more time healing. But I thought I could handle it.

I was wrong. And I was no closer to becoming the man I wanted to be. If anything, I was moving in the wrong direction. That's when I got brave enough to admit it. I was still me, and I did not like it one bit. I began writing it down, believing that somehow that would help me figure it out.

I moved back to Atlanta and had the major health scare I described earlier. Then I got divorced. Then I was diagnosed with depression. Then my car was rear-ended and totaled. A concussion. A growing pain-pill habit. Financial trouble. And then my girlfriend—the one I've been talking about all through this book—we broke up. And it was my fault. Old patterns of foolish behavior, careless talk, bad boundaries, all combined with a brain injury and a recently diagnosed mental illness. I can be a difficult man to love, and she ran out of patience and sent me packing. Same song, different verse.

None of this was in the script.

THE ME I AM SUPPOSED TO BE

It seemed as if the harder I pushed to become the me I was supposed to be, the further away it fled. Finally, I collapsed in a heap. After all these years, I was still me. And I was beginning to hate me. I'm writing this in a hotel in Augusta, Georgia. Who knows where I'll be by the time you're reading this. Probably still in the larvae stage.

I may never achieve butterfly status, but I'm growing. I can feel it every now and then. I see something differently than I used to see it. My opinion on some culture-warrior issue shifts. I find my heart longing for something I used to avoid and avoiding something I used to long for. My appetites adjust. More and more things are shifting in the direction of grace and away from judgment. I'm moving toward love, toward forgiveness, toward mercy, toward hope.

I refuse to believe I'm becoming more naïve in my old age. I think I may finally be coming to see the kinds of things that caused Jesus to say, "The kingdom has broken in and is expanding. It's so close you can reach out and touch it with your hand. And one day, the whole world will be overcome by it."

So many things change, and there's so little that is actually ours to control. I cannot, for example, control how you'll respond to what I've written here. You may choose to fall on your knees and cry out to God. Or you may choose to write me off as a heretic. You may find yourself thinking differently about things. Or you may go about your business as usual.

I can't control you. I can't control my circumstances—no matter how hard I try. I can only control myself (and sometimes not even that). I can work on controlling the things I say and do. Beyond that, who knows what tomorrow may bring?

Well, at the risk of stating the obvious, God does. He knew what would happen, which conversations would take place and find their way into this book, how you would respond to all of this, where I would be living. He knew all of this when I first ran the idea of this book past my agent. God chooses to reveal what he reveals, and I'm relatively sure he's got his reasons.

One thing I do know: I am not the same man I was when this process began. Things are different. I think I'm more myself than I was. I like to think I'm more like Jesus than I was (I'm not one of those people who assume the two are mutually exclusive). As painful as this process has been, the pain is redemptive. God has used that pain to forge compassion in me, to form a stronger character, a Christlikeness that wasn't there before, or at least wasn't there as consistently as it is now.

I know that I'm not who I was, and I also know that I'm not yet who I will be. God is in the process of transforming me, a process that won't be done this side of eternity. He's in control, and he has my best interests at heart. If I ever doubt that, I'll just pick up this book. Or call Bill.

Thomas Merton was a prolific letter writer. He carried on extensive correspondence with people from all over the world. For most of the 1960s, Merton had a running conversation with a woman named Etta Gullick, an Anglican professor who was teaching prayer and theology courses at Oxford. They wrote about many things, including her struggles with God's love. One time, Etta explained that she just didn't love God. Merton's response was a true gem. He wrote: "You say you do not think you love God, and that is probably perfectly true. But what matters is that God loves you, isn't it? If we had to rely on *our* love, where would we be?"

This is the point, and it does not get any pointier than this. God's love is stronger than my best efforts or intentions, stronger than my worst days, stronger than my feeble attempts at self-improvement, stronger than my failing and flailing tendency to self-sabotage. God's care for me does not waiver based on my emotional or chemical imbalances. It does not ebb just because I'm mad or depressed or I wish my life were different. Lean into that love, and remember: the One who began this good work in you is going to see it through to completion.

EPILOGUE

Most of my life has been one big race to get the things I thought I needed to have in order to be happy. I needed more money so I could finally do what I want when I want. I needed more success, so I could feel fulfilled and proud of myself. I needed more connections, so I could feel loved and valued. Mostly, I ended up with more distractions so I could avoid the fact that I was miserable with myself.

I'd trick myself into thinking I was making progress and pushing myself. But when I was doing all of this and supposedly stretching myself, in actuality I was really pretending that happiness was just over the next ridge. Happiness was always something that I had almost achieved. I'd probably get there tomorrow, or the day after that, or the day after that . . .

The truth I'm coming to learn is that nothing will ever bring me joy if I attach happiness to something just out of my reach. In my experience, when I finally get those things, I feel emptier than I did before because I am reminded that there is a void in me that things cannot fulfill—only self-acceptance can. If I'm never happy where I am, I'll never be happy when I get where I'm going. At least, not long-term.

I'm going to go out on a limb and say that I'm not the only person here who feels like this. I bet some of you have also attached too much of your hope and energy to something you want—a job, a relationship, an award. Your entire life can begin to revolve around achieving that one thing—all your thoughts and conversations and activities—all aimed at that one, elusive thing.

And then you get it, and it feels really great . . . for a moment. It feels like it was all worth it . . . for a moment. But it never lasts. It's not long before you realize there is another level you could get to. You convince yourself that this isn't enough; you now have to have that. Why settle for being a butterfly, when you could be an eagle or an airplane or a rocket ship?

There's always a next step in your evolution. And that can become maddening. You think that if you can just get to the next stage, your life will be complete. But there's another stage after that one, and another after that one. You want it so badly, until you get it, and then you see the next horizon, and you want that. The object of your desire is always shifting to the next level.

There are two pieces to desire, though, and I've just recently come to see something that I think might be really important. There is the thing I desire, the thing upon which I fix my gaze, the brass ring, the gold star. I want it, and I want it bad. I think I might die if I don't get it. That's how badly I want that one thing.

There is that one thing, and then there is the thing that makes me want that one thing. That's a whole other thing—maybe a more important thing than the first thing.

If I get the gold star, I will feel validated. If I get the girl, I will feel complete and whole. If I get the promotion, I will feel respected. If I get the bigger house, I will feel envied by my brother-in-law who bought that foreclosure place with the gigantic swimming pool. People will know that I'm a big shot if I drive that car or wear those shoes.

I think the thing that I want is the girl, the promotion, the house, the car, or the shoes. But I don't really want the thing I think I want as much as I want the thing that makes me want the thing. I want validation. I want to feel complete and whole. I want respect. I want people to envy me. I want them to think I'm a big shot.

There's the thing I want, and then there's the thing that makes me want it. I usually chase the former, but when I get it, I feel dissatisfied because what I really want is the latter.

This is true in nearly every aspect of my life, and I think it might help explain what I see as some of the themes that have surfaced in this book.

I want to be different, to be better than I currently am. I want to grow. I want to change. But the truth of the matter is, I am different, I have grown, I'm constantly changing. I'm better than I was. I'm more mature, wiser, stronger.

And it's never enough.

Because maybe I don't want to change as much as I want to want to change. Surely, I'm more like Jesus at forty-seven than I was a twenty-seven. I've grown in the areas of love, joy, peace, patience, kindness, goodness, faithfulness, gentleness, and self-control. I'm more resilient now than I was, more humble, more generous, more gracious, more merciful. Anyone who has known me for that long can tell you. I'm a better person now than I used to be.

I'm not sure how one could go about doing this, but if an objective measurement could be set up to score someone in those Christ-like virtues, the forty-seven-year-old me blows away the thirty-seven-year-old me. I've lived too much, gone through too much hell, I've read and studied and listened to too many wise people to still be stuck as the exact same person I was ten or twenty years ago. Heraclitus said, "No man ever steps in the same river twice, for it's not the same river and he's not the same man." Water flows. Time passes. We all change. The general, overarching patterns may still be there, but the specific day-in-and-day-out stuff? It's changed. C. S. Lewis puts these words into Prince Caspian's mouth, "Isn't it funny how day by day nothing changes but when you look back everything is different?"

But the more mature I become, the more aware of my immaturity I become. The closer I get to the me I want to be, the greater the gap between there and where I am now appears.

Perhaps this is why I am drawn to stillness these days. In the stillness, I recognize first that I am different. Second, stillness allows me to confess that I'm still not satisfied. Finally, stillness helps me to see that what I truly want is to know that I am not there yet, not done cooking, not finished transforming, that I am still me—just a slightly modified and slightly upgraded version of me. I'm me 2.0 with a new patch that fixes some of the bugs that were in the old system but, inevitably, has new bugs of its own (or new versions of the old ones). Like the software running on my computer, there are constantly going to be updates for newer and improved versions. What a sad day it would be to look at yourself and call yourself a "grown-up"—as if you're done growing up.

I hope I never get there. When I stop growing, I start dying.

I want to know that as long as I'm conscious, I can always get better.

And so, what I want more than transformation is the knowledge that transformation is still necessary, that transformation is always possible, that it is still constantly in process. I have the vision, the intention, and the means. But there is no final destination, no finish line, no point at which I can say, "At last, I'm done." I will be in flux for the rest of my existence, and that is a good thing. If that's what I want most—the thing that makes me want the thing that I think I want most—and it's present to such an extent that it bothers me . . . well . . . then I already have what I want most.

And that means there's no good reason for me not to be happy right now.

Yes, things are hard. I won't deny that. I know pain and suffering, relationships come apart, my back is killing me, my brain is damaged, my liver hurts, bills keep rolling in even though I don't have money to pay them, things are not the way they're supposed to be. Still . . . I can be content because I have what I want most—which is the knowledge that things aren't the way they're supposed to be and the willingness to make changes that will get me closer to the way things are supposed to be.

It's unrealistic to think I'll ever reach a point where I stop wanting more or that I'll reach a point of complete and utter satisfaction with the status quo. That's actually a positive thing. When people are dissatisfied, that's when they innovate, they try new things and explore new possibilities.

If I were satisfied with my life, I never would have written this book. I'm pretty sure that if I can summon the strength to sit still and embrace the idea that I have everything I need right now, I can start loving both the me I currently am and the me I am becoming.

Now, if you'll excuse me, I have to go celebrate the fact that I'm still me.